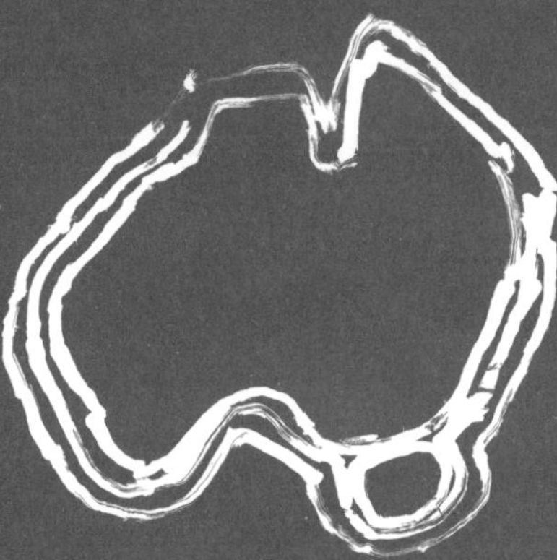

Manta Nganampa
Tjukurtjara Munu Kunpu
alatjitu Ku Tjupangk Ngurpangku
Patu Upani Ku kunpu
ngarannyi
Manta .

Tjina
Tjunku Wiya
nganampa
Tjukurpangka

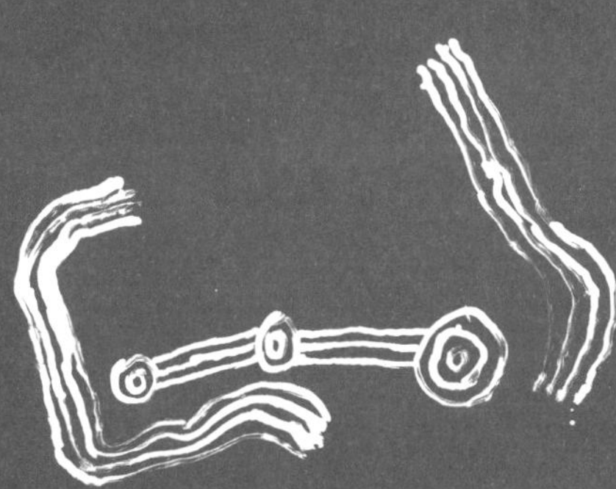

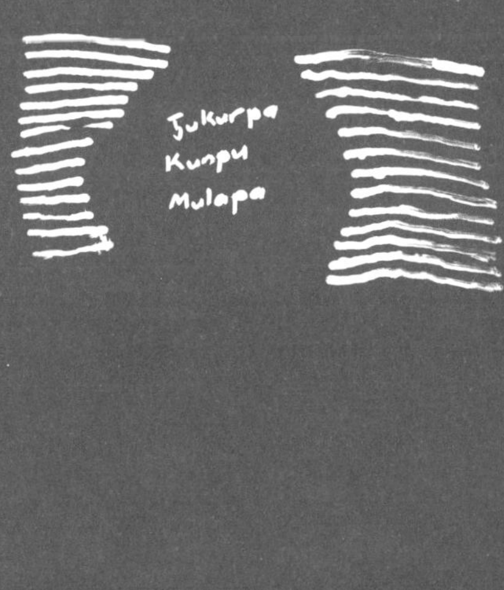

Aboriginal and Torres Strait Islander people are advised that this book contains images and words of people who have passed away.

Kulinmaya!

Keep listening, everybody!

Mumu Mike Williams held vast knowledge of his country and culture. He had authority to speak as he has spoken in this book. His authority to speak accorded with the Law of the country. It rested with him as a senior man for certain traditions of the country and as the holder of stories for a certain place. He expressed his lived experience and knowledge in this book. It contains elements, aspects and learnings of the author. Some cultural knowledge is known to many. The author has shown care not to include knowledge that should be known only by some. The author said all cultural knowledge belongs to the people of Anangu Pitjantjatjara Yankunytjatjara lands and that according to culture and tradition certain persons have standing and authority for specific places. Authority for certain places passes from generation to generation.

First published by Allen & Unwin in 2019

Most of the historical image research for *Kulinmaya!* was conducted through Ara Irititja, an Anangu-owned, community-based archive. All historical images identified with 'AI' numbers in this book are from collections donated to Ara Irititja. Ara Irititja has a long history of repatriating digital material back to Anangu using interactive software.

For further acknowledgements see pp. 209–11 Every effort has been made to contact copyright holders. The publisher welcomes contact with any copyright holders not here acknowledged.

Allen & Unwin
83 Alexander Street
Crows Nest NSW 2065
Australia
Phone: (61 2) 8425 0100
Email: info@allenandunwin.com
Web: www.allenandunwin.com

NATIONAL LIBRARY OF AUSTRALIA
A catalogue record for this book is available from the National Library of Australia

ISBN 978 1 76052 442 5

For teaching resources, explore www.allenandunwin.com/resources/for-teachers

Cover design by Mumu Mike Williams and Joanna Hunt
Text design by Joanna Hunt
Set in 11.5pt Esta by Joanna Hunt

This book was printed in April 2019 by C&C Offset Printing Co. Ltd, China.

10 9 8 7 6 5 4 3 2 1

FSC www.fsc.org MIX Paper from responsible sources FSC® C008047

Mimili Maku

Australian Government
Indigenous Languages and Arts
Supported through the Australian Government's Indigenous Languages and Arts program

GORDON DARLING FOUNDATION Publication sponsor

Kulinmaya!

Keep listening, everybody!

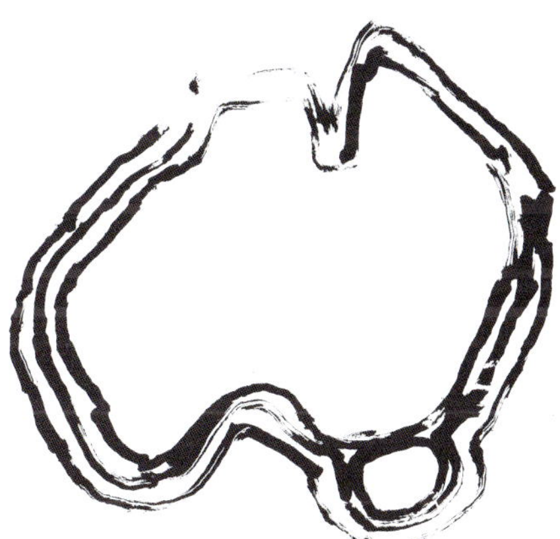

Mumu Mike Williams

English translation by Linda Rive

ALLEN&UNWIN
SYDNEY • MELBOURNE • AUCKLAND • LONDON

AUSTRALIA
THE NATIONAL GEOGRAPHIC MAGAZINE
JACKEROO
Care Quip

Contents

Introduction 1

Irititja 3
Early life

Nganampa Tjukurpa 31
Our Tjukurpa

Canvas munu ku<u>l</u>a<u>t</u>a 49
Canvas and spears

'I'm still making ku<u>l</u>a<u>t</u>a every day' by Sammy Dodd 56

Walkatjunanyi 73
Writing as artform

Aa<u>l</u>piri nyuwana 89
Working on mailbags

Ku<u>l</u>a<u>t</u>a 121
The old men and their spears are guarding their culture

Itjinpiri 137
Itjinpiri past and present

Wa<u>r</u>u pitjantja 189
The way fire was returned

Australia, palya? 192
Essay by Hetti Kemerre Perkins

Contributors 200
Glossary 206
List of works 208
Acknowledgements 210
Index 212

Mumu Mike Williams was a senior Pitjantjatjara artist based in the community of Mimili on the Anangu Pitjantjatjara Yankunytjatjara (APY) Lands in the north-west of South Australia. Born in 1952 at Inturtjanu, Williams saw his world, and the world around him, change in many ways throughout his lifetime.

Mimili Community lies within the beautiful Everard Ranges, around 488 kilometres south-west of Alice Springs. At one time known as Everard Park, a cattle station, the area was returned to Aboriginal ownership through the 1981 *APY Land Rights Act*. Today, Mimili is home to about 250 Pitjantjatjara and Yankunytjatjara people who refer to themselves as Anangu.

Williams was an elder and ngangkari (traditional healer), pastor and politician, activist and artist, passionate about passing his knowledge on to future generations. He was one of the directors at Mimili Maku Arts, a vibrant contemporary art studio led by a strong board of Anangu, supporting artists across different disciplines such as painting, photography, new media – and most recently, publishing. Williams is renowned across the country for his provocative art practice repurposing Commonwealth documents, mailbags and maps using Pitjantjatjara text and raw brush marks to boldly state his claim. His practice is a tribute to the time he spent advocating for issues like governance, sustainable land management, the protection of sacred heritage sites, and the rights of traditional owners.

Williams always remained very clear about the intent behind his works, offering them not only as a warning to the Commonwealth, whose actions post the 1981 APY Lands handback continued to concern him, but also as an opportunity to inform and share the rich knowledge contained within Anangu culture. In this spirit, the realisation of *Kulinmaya!* was a longstanding dream of his.

Mimili Maku Arts

Pages vi–vii: Mumu Mike Williams' home of Mimili Community.

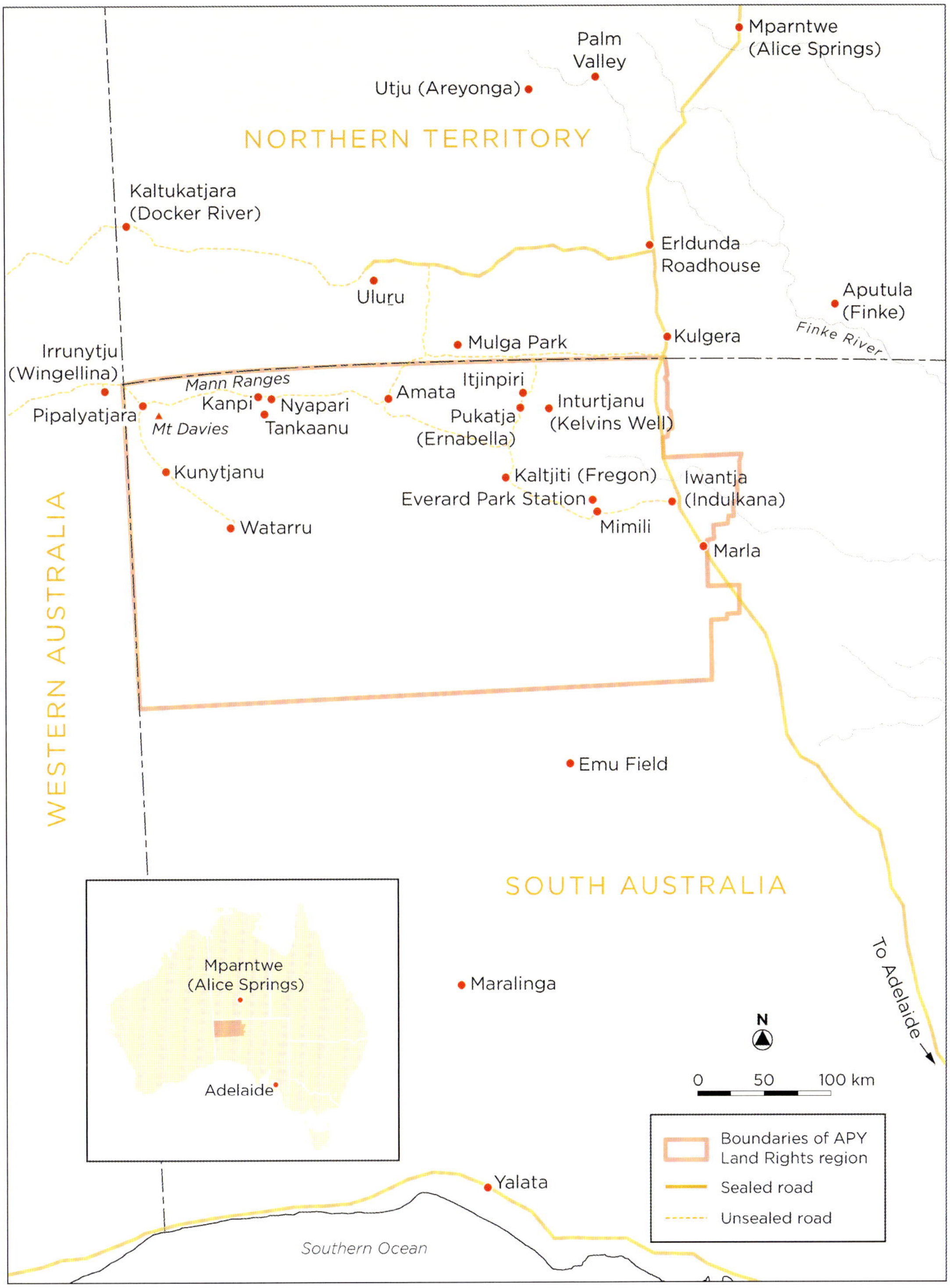
Mparntwe
(Alice Springs)
Palm
Valley
Utju (Areyonga)
NORTHERN TERRITORY
Kaltukatjara
(Docker River)
Erldunda
Roadhouse
Uluru
Aputula
(Finke)
Finke River
Kulgera
Mulga Park
Irrunytju
(Wingellina)
Mann Ranges
Itjinpiri
Amata
Kanpi
Nyapari
Pipalyatjara
Mt Davies
Tankaanu
Pukatja
(Ernabella)
Inturtjanu
(Kelvins Well)
Kunytjanu
Kaltjiti (Fregon)
Iwantja
(Indulkana)
Everard Park Station
Watarru
Mimili
Marla
WESTERN AUSTRALIA
Emu Field
SOUTH AUSTRALIA
Mparntwe
(Alice Springs)
Adelaide
Maralinga
To Adelaide
N
0
50
100 km
Boundaries of APY
Land Rights region
Sealed road
Unsealed road
Yalata
Southern Ocean

Introduction

Ngayulu nyaaku kulini, nyiringka Tjukurpa tjunkunytjikitja, munu ngayulu mukuringanyi tjilpi tjuta – tjilpi mulapa tjuta – kuranytju ngaranytjaku munu yangapala, wati yangapala tjuta nintintjaku.

I hope my book will work in the same way the Tjukurpa was handed down to me by the oldest of the elders – the ones who have lived the longest – and help to teach the young men.

Tjukurpa nganampa mantangka ngarantja tjuta. Tjukurpa wara wangkanyi. Tjana kulintjaku munu tjukurpa wara tjunkunytjaku munu mutu-mutu palya. Palu wara – main one.

Our lands are covered with Tjukurpa sites all over. Tjukurpa is a long story. If I could write it all down I would, but for this book I have to keep it short, which is acceptable. But the main Tjukurpa story is epic.

Tjukurpa nyangatja kunpu. Kunpu, like kunpu ngarantjaku. Tjitji malatja malatja tjutaku. Nyitayira tjutaku. Kungka tjutaku. Tjukurpa nganampa manta nyangangka ngaranyi pulka. Ka ngayulu mukuringanyi Tjukurpa nyanga palunya nyiringka tjunkunytjikitjangku, kulintjaku.

Tjukurpa is powerful. Forceful, it is like a powerful force. It is there for children of the future. For the boys. For the girls. Our landscape is rich and diverse with powerful Tjukurpa. This is what I want to convey in this book.

Irititja

Early life

Ngayuku ini Mumu Mike Williams. Ngayulu iṯi wirkanu. 15 February 1952. Ngura Inturtjanu. Kelvins Well. Puṯingka. Tjiipi kanyinyangka. Ngunytju mamangka. Kalanya ngayuku mama Yilkunya munu ngayuku ngunytju Maringkanya.

My name is Mumu Mike Williams. I was born 15 February 1952 at Inturtjanu, Kelvins Well. In the bush. My mother and father were shepherds there. My father's name was Yilku Mulayangu Harry Williams, and my mother's name was Maringka Williams.

Tjiipi kanyilpai, ngayuku ngunytju, ka ngayuli iṯi ngaringu tjiipingka, tjiipiku ngurangka, like Inturtjanu, Black Hill numpa three-ngka itingka. Yaaṯangka tjunu, ka ngayulu iṯi ngaringu nyara palula. Ngaḻtutjara.

I was born at a sheep camp, where the sheep were yarded, at Inturtjanu, which is not far from Black Hill Number Three. At that big sheep yard, that's where I was born, right there. Ngaḻtutjara (bless)!

Ngayulu Pitjantjatjara wangkapai. Ngayuku ngunytju Pipalyatjaranya ngurara. Ka ngayuku mama Tankaanunya ngurara. Kanpi area. Amatanya wiya. Warburton, Areyonga munu Ernabellanya kutju.

I speak Pitjantjatjara. My mother was from Pipalyatjara. My father was from Tankaanu, from the Kanpi area. There was no Amata community then, just Warburton, Areyonga and Ernabella.

Page 2: Mumu Mike Williams' father Yilku Mulayangu Harry Williams throwing a spear at a mock kangaroo during the Ernabella Mission sports day in 1952.
Photo: Collection Frank & Mary Bennett, A<u>r</u>a Irititja (AI-0005324)

Above: Mumu Mike Williams (right) and his cousin-brother Tjilari Edwards rounding up sheep near the Ernabella Mission shearing shed, June 1963.
Photo: Collection Ruary Bucknall, A<u>r</u>a Irititja (AI–0026744)

Ngayulu anu Ernabella ku. Ngayunya katingu. School-ngka tjarpangu. Ngayuku teacher Nancy Nicholson munu Lucy Turner. Paluru tjana teacher nyinangi. Ngananana nintiringangi Pitjantjatjara, ngurangka Pitjantjatjara wangkangi, wiltjangka. Wiltjangka, mamalu, ngunytjulu. Pitjantjatjara walkatjunanyi, readamilani.

Later, I went to Ernabella. My parents took me there. I started school. My teachers were Nancy Nicholson and Lucy Turner. We were learning the Pitjantjatjara language, which was my first language, spoken at home in our wiltja. We learnt writing and reading in Pitjantjatjara.

Kuulitja tjuta nganana kuulangka malanka katipai, tjiramilala *rrrruuuu* ka nganana katipai, ngura kutjupa kutu, like Kunma Piti, Balfours Well, Putitja, Puntitjata, Wamikata or Itjinpiri. Nganana katipai, ka ngananyanya ungkupai, missionary-ngku five dollar, enough for arintji-ku [oranges]. Haha.

After school, we schoolchildren would go shearing, *rrrruuuu*, and then we would take the sheep back to their sheep camps, such as to Kunma Piti, Balfours Well, Putitja, Puntitjata, Wamikata or Itjinpiri. We would herd them back and then the missionary would give us five dollars, enough for oranges. Haha.

Opposite top: Ernabella Mission when Mumu Mike was little – the ration shed and store are on the left, the church is beyond and in between is the art centre. November 1959.
Photo: Collection Ian Spalding, Ara Irititja (AI–0026281)

Opposite bottom: Mumu Mike's father, Yilku Mulayangu Harry Williams (in checked shirt), with family and women spinning wool near Ernabella, c1964.
Photo: Collection David Driver, Ara Irititja (AI-0017265)

Ngayuku ngura
My birthplace

Iyukuṯanya ngayuku ngura. Iyukuṯanya, Inturtjanunya nguraṟa. Minyma Kutjara kangkuṟuṟara. Iyukuṯanya pitjangi Ernabella nguṟu. Ernabella airstrip-ngka itingka anu, Inturtjanula kutu. From there ngalya pitjangu munu nyinangi, piṟanpa kutjara, apu kutjara. Palm Valley munu Finke River, ngalya pitjangu munu panya Old Timersta nguṟu tjarpangu, nganala kutu, Bungalowla kutu. Minymaku Tjukurpa. Old Bungalow.

My birthplace is the Two Women Tjukurpa, Iyukuta. They are there at Inturtjanu. These Two Women are two sisters. They were journeying from near where Ernabella airstrip is today, to Inturtjanu. From there they journeyed towards Palm Valley and the Finke River, where there are two white hills. From there they travelled to Old Timers, and from there to the Bungalow in Alice Springs. The Old Bungalow.

Ka minyma kutjupa tjuṯa Irrunytjula nguṟu pitjangu kutjara kutjupa tjuṯa. Ka minyma kutjupa tjuṯa nyanga nguṟu anu Wave Hill kutu. Watiku wiya nyanga paluṟu minyma tjuṯaku. Arrernte, Warlpiri, tjuṯaku.

Many other ancestral women also travelled in pairs from Irrunytju and numerous other places. Two women also travelled from Alice Springs to Wave Hill. These stories do not belong to the men, they belong to the women, Arrernte women and Walpiri women, too.

Kelvins Well. Inturtjanu. Tjiipiku ngura. Inturtjanu. Kenmorenya itingka, Ernabella, Black Hill, Donald's Well. Nguṟurpa. Road Kenmorela kutu ngalya ngarinyi. Ngayulu kanyini Iyukutaku Tjukurpa. Ka tjana tjawaṉu, Inturtjanunya road palyalpai tjuṯangku, road palyantjaku.

Inturtjanu is also known as Kelvins Well. It is not far from Kenmore, Ernabella, Black Hill and Donald's Well. It is there in the middle. It is not far from the Kenmore Road.

This is where I hold my Iyukuta Tjukurpa. But they have been digging there at Inturtjanu; the road builders have been digging there for material to build roads.

Mumu Mike Williams was born in the bush near this place, Inturtjanu (Kelvins Well), in 1952, four years after this photo was taken.
Photo: Collection Frank & Mary Bennett, Ara Irititja (AI-0015558)

Ngayulu kulangka panya nyinangi nikiti, panya titjangku pailpai wiya, ulytjangka tjarpanytja wiya. Ka ngayulu, munu ngayulu mukuringkupai Englisha nintiringkunytjaku, ka titjangku watjanu, 'Wiya, nyuntu nintiringanyi nyuntumpa wangkaku. Munu nyuntu nikiti nyinanyi ngula kunta wiyaku wangkanytjaku.' Ka haha nyara palunya kulinu, 'Ai mulapa ngayunya nintiningi titjangku, wangka ngayuku numpa one, Pitjantjatjara. Numpa two, English.'

When I went to school, I went there naked. Our teachers would not let us wear clothes [for skin health reasons]. I very much wanted to learn the English language but my teachers said to me, 'No, you must first learn your own language. You must remain naked and you must learn to speak up with confidence.' I listened to them and realised, 'Ah, I see, my teachers are educating me in my own language first. Number one, Pitjantjatjara. Number two, English.'

Ka wirunya alatjitu. Ka ngayulu ngula tjapinu, 'Ai, ngayulu mukuringanyi Englishaku nintiringkunytjikitja, kulangka.' Ka watjanu, 'Wiya. Numpa one nyuntumpa. Wangka nyuntumpaku nintiringanyi munu kututungku kanyini.'

So it all worked out well. After a while I asked, 'Hey, I want to learn English now.' Again, I was told, 'No.

Number one, you must be fluent and literate in your own language. You must learn it and carry it in your heart and soul for the rest of your life.'

'If nyuntu Englishaku nintiringanyi nyuntu, wangka nyuntumpa watarkurinyi, putu kulini: Wangka ngayuku yaaltji? Ka paluru ngananya, Miss Nicholson, titja [Nancy Sheppard, nee Nicholson].

'If you learn English first, you will forget your own language, and then you'll be asking later, where did my language go?' [Enacting the words of one who had lost their language]. Miss Nicholson was my teacher then [Nancy Sheppard, nee Nicholson].

Ernabella School, c1958. Nancy Sheppard (nee Nicholson) is in the school doorway; Lucy Turner is at far left.
Photo: Collection Bruce Edenborough, Aṟa Irititja (AI-0009588)

Ngayulu titja tjuṯa nyinangi maṟu tjuṯa, like Lucy Turner. Kutjupara titja panya nyaa tjuṯa nyinanyi, Pitjantjatjara nintilpai. Palula nguṟu ngayulu kuwari nyanga tjukurpa ngayukungku walkatjunanyi Pitjantjatjarangku ka kutjupangku translatamilala walkatjunanyi, tjana ritamilala kulinytjaku, ai, tjukurpa nyangatja. Kutjara, wangka kutjara, kuṉpu.

I also had a number of Aṉangu teachers, such as Lucy Turner. Our teachers would be teaching us in Pitjantjatjara. Ever since then I have been able to read and write stories in Pitjantjatjara, as well as do translations, so that people can read documents in both languages and truly understand the right messages. So I'm fluent now in the two languages.

Weekend ankupai donkey-ngka tjitji tjuṯa paṯu. Piṟanpangku pailpai, 'Waḻingka para ngaṟantja wiya. Waḻingka itingka wiya. Puṯi kutu ara!' Nyiṯayira tjuṯa ankupai, tjuṯinpya tjara, rabbit-aku.

On the weekends, we children would ride out on our donkeys. The mission staff would send us away, 'Do not hang around the mission buildings. Do not come near any of the buildings. Go out bush!' So we boys would all go out together with our clubs, hunting rabbits.

Kungka tjuṯa nyara nyakula ungkupai. Tiṉka. Ngiṉtaka. Iḻi, kampuṟarpa, wiriny-wirinypa, kulypurpa, paluṟu tjana, maku kuḻu. Mai puṯitjangka. Ngayuku ngunytjungku pauḻpai, wanguṉu munu kunakanti, like damper. Mai wiṟu.

We'd hunt and give the girls some of our meat, goanna and perentie lizard. We'd also eat figs, desert raisins, bush tomatoes, wild gooseberries and all those wild bush foods, as well as witchetty grubs. My mother would bake wild bush seeds and grains like woollybutt and wild millet into a kind of damper. It is delicious food.

Opposite top: Mumu Mike's family before his birth, Ernabella, August 1943.
Photo: Collection Len Young family, Aṟa Irititja (AI-0185755)

Opposite bottom: Mumu Mike's mother, Maringka, with his older brother, Atira Atira Michael, in Ernabella, August 1943 (detail).
Photo: Collection Len Young family, Aṟa Irititja (AI-0185752)

Mai ratjina ngayulu nyakupai, ngaṟapai. Ngayuku mamangku, ngunytjungku paluṟu pula mantjilpai. Kutjupaṟa papa miṟi tjana sellamilalpai.

I also used to see my father and mother getting rations from the ration shed. Sometimes they would sell their dingo scalps there.

Nganaṉa para ngaṟapai tjina, donkey-ngka, kamuḻangka, paṯu. Kutjupaṟa ankupai Mulga Park, nyaa kutu, like Itjinpiri, Youngs Well, kulangka ila, one week. Christmas holidays nganaṉa paṯu ankupai, uwankara. Kutjupa tjuṯa Kenmore-ku, kutjupa tjuṯa Fregonta nguṟu ankupai, kutjupa tjuṯa Mulga Park, kutjupa tjuṯa Amata, Pipalyatjara ku. Waḻi wiya ngaṟanyangka.

We would walk great distances around the country on foot, or riding donkeys or camels. Sometimes we'd go to Mulga Park, or just to Youngs Well for the week, so as to be close to school. During the Christmas holidays, everybody would go a long way away. Some would go through Kenmore, others would go via the Fregon area, others to Mulga Park, or through Amata, and others would go to Pipalyatjara. This is back when community buildings didn't exist.

Opposite top: Mumu Mike (at right) and his cousin-brother Tjilari Edwards riding donkeys in Ernabella, June 1963.
Photo: Collection Ruary Bucknall, Aṟa Irititja (AI-0026586)

Opposite bottom: Aṉangu lined up at the store and ration shed at Ernabella, 1960.
Photo: Collection Nancy Sheppard (Nicholson), Aṟa Irititja (AI-0016479)

Pages 16–17: Mumu Mike's parents, Yilku Mulayangu Harry Williams and Maringka Williams, at Ernabella, ready to go on holiday, August 1962.
Photo: Collection Shirley Gudgeon (Hill), Aṟa Irititja (AI-0006387)

Katipai tjitji nyakunytjaku. Uwa ngayunya katingu Nyapari area, Kanpinya tjanampa area, Murputjanya. Tjukula kutu, puli katu. Pulka. Mount Daviesta nguru. Pipalyatjarala nguru, Kunytjanu.

The children were taken in order to show them their country. I was taken to the Nyapari and Kanpi area, to our traditional country along the Mann Ranges. We'd go to the rockholes, up on the mountainside. It is huge there. We'd travel via Mount Davies, Pipalyatjara and Kunytjanu.

Ngananana tjina ankupai. Wiru. Paku wiya. Ipilypa. Pukulpa, pika wiya, pikatjararingkunytja wiya. Ngananana Nyaparila nyinapai, munu ngananana ankupai. Kala mala pitjapai schoolakutu, right time. Three or four weeks ngananana ankupai. Wiru.

We walked everywhere. It was beautiful. We never got tired. We were fit and healthy. Nobody got sick or injured. We would stay around the Nyapari area, and then move again. After our holidays, we'd return to school at the right time. We would go travelling for three or four weeks at a time. It was wonderful.

Opposite top: Anangu on holiday, travelling the country – trading dingo scalps and picking up rations at Yulpartji, August 1958.
Photo: Collection Bruce Edenborough, Ara Irititja (AI-0009513)

Opposite bottom: Trading dingo scalps at Yulpartji, 21 August 1958. Frank Young is looking around on the donkey in the foreground, and the two women nearby are his older mother Amanyi Young (left) and Nyunutja George, his younger mother.
Photo: Collection Bruce Edenborough, Ara Irititja (AI-0009506)

Ngayuku warka
My work

Ngayulu panya iriti ngayulu tjaatarira warkarinyi, like pulukangka ngurpa, palu ngayulu nitiringanyi panya, ngura nganala, Kenmore-la. Nyara palula ngayulu nintiringkula nintiringkula...munu nyanytju panya ngananana ngura kutjupakutu anu, William Creek. Ngayulu warkarinyi, nyara palula, yangapala four. Ka William Creek-a-nguru malaku anu Finke-ku. Finkela nguru Alice Springs. Alice Springs-ala nguru piruku anu, patu.

When I first started working, I had no idea about bullocks, but I began to learn stock work at Kenmore Park Station. It was there that my knowledge and experience grew, until I was able to ride horses all the way to William Creek. I worked in a team of four youngfellas. From William Creek we rode to Finke, then from Finke we rode to Alice Springs. From Alice Springs we rode to a station even further away.

Ka puluka tjuta kura tjuta, yuruwilya wara. Palu ngananananya pailpai, wati tjilpi tjuta nyinangi, ninti tjuta. 'Ai, patu ngarama, nyanytju wakanytjaku tawara.' Ka yangapala tjuta ngananana warkara warkara nintiringu.

Bullocks can be really dangerous with their long, sharp horns. The old highly experienced stockmen would warn us, 'Hey, make sure you keep your distance from them, in case they gouge your horses.' After experiences like that we youngfellas became experts ourselves.

Malaku pitjangu Anapalaku. Munu ngananana tawarangka ngaripai. Munu tawara-nguru ali pakara ankupai munula tjaataringu, ngayulu palyaningi bricks. Tjuminta panya tjuta ngalya pakani, tjinguru five hundred or six hundred, brick tjuta ka panya kuwarilta tjuminta nyuntu nyangangi? Anapalala tjuwangka panya? Ngananana palyanytja. Ka warka wiru tjuta.

Afterwards we returned to Ernabella and the tawara camp (segregation camp). We lived in the tawara camp, waking up early to start work, making bricks. We mixed cement and we made five or six hundred bricks. Have you seen the cement bricks in Ernabella? On Ernabella store? We made those bricks. It was really good work.

Wati kutjungku wangkangu, wati tjilpingku, tjamu nganampangku, paluru aalpiringku wangkangi, 'Nyuntu tjamu tjutangka kulira. Nyuntu wanka nyinanyi, manta nyangangka. Palu nyuntu ngananya kulira wantinyi, nyuntu too young ilunyi.' Ka ngayulu kulini, 'Ai, ai, ai, ai, mulapa. Tjukurpa nyangatja mulapa.'

One old man, our grandfather, called out to us during the aalpiri speeches,

'Listen to your grandfather's advice. You are living on this land. If you don't heed your elders you will die young.' I would listen to him and think, 'Yes, yes, yes, yes, true. He is telling the truth.'

Munu ngayulu tawarangka ngaripai, tawarangka nyinapai, pukulpa nyinapai. Ka mulapa, yangapala tjuta wiyaringanyi, tjamuku tjanampa tjukurpa kulira ankula wantima.

Sleeping in the tawara camp, sleeping and living there, I was happy and content. But it is true what the old man said, those youngfellas who have abandoned traditional principles and not listened to their grandfathers have died young.

Ka ngayulu nyinapai nganala, Adelaide. Adelaide-la ngayulu nyinapai ka an̲angu kutjupa tjut̲a nintiningi, ka palur̲u tjana tawaratjangka tjarpangu, liritjaku tjunu, munu palur̲u tjana anu, panya nyangaku, casino kutu tjikinytjikitja. Ka ngayulu kulini, 'Ai, yaaltji-yaaltji?' Palur̲u tjana mal̲aku pitjangu ngurakutu, ka ngayulu al̲i in the morning ngayulu wangkangu, panya, 'Nganampa kaltja wiya palatja. Nganampa ar̲a wiya. Nganampa tjukurpa wiya.' Tjukurpa nganampa upan̲i, nganampa. Ka nyanga palunya ngayulu kulini.

I often stay in Adelaide. In Adelaide, I have watched my people learn different things, such as putting on smart trousers and ties, and going off to the casino to drink. And I'm there thinking, 'What for?' When they come home I speak to them early in the morning. I say to them, 'The casino is not our culture. It is not our way. It is not our cultural heritage.' It only weakens our cultural identity. That's what I believe.

Opposite: Brickmaking for buildings in Ernabella, 1952. This is like the work Mumu Mike did to build the store in Ernabella.
Photos: Collection Bill & Allison Elliott, Ar̲a Irititja (AI-0004560) & (AI-0004560)

Tawara
The tawara segregation camp

Some time Christmas-ngka mala tjana business startaripai. Ngayulu tawara kutu, nyiinka kutu. Nyiinka tjuta patu nyinapai. Ka ngayulu tjanala kutu, 'Ankula mai mantjilpai tjanampa.' Kala ungkupai mai nyiinka tjuta kutu. Putuya ankupai minyma tjuta. Tjana patu nyinanyi, tawaritja tjuta.

Some time after Christmas, men's ceremonial business would start up. I'd be going back and forth to the tawara camp. The pre-initiates would be camped a long way away. Nyiinka pre-initiates must always be camped separately. I would go and visit them there. 'Here, carry this food out to them,' I'd be told. We would give the pre-initiates their food. Women were not allowed to do this task.

Ngayulu watiringu kulu.

In time, I too became a man.

Ngananа nyiinkangka nyinapai munu ngananа anyway ankunytja wiya ngura kutu. Kami nganampangku pailpai, 'Wiya ara! Nyuntu mai kati!' Ka ngananа nyinapai tawarangka. Tawara. Tawarangka nyinapai pukulpa. Pala palulangka wati tjilpi tjutangku nyakupai. Uwa inmaku pakalpai, munu tjana wirura kanyilpai. Nintilpai tjitji tjuta.

For the duration of our nyiinka pre-initiate stage, we stayed in a certain place and were not allowed to return home. Our grandmothers had warned us, 'No, you must stay away! You must hunt for your own food!' So we stayed away in the tawara segregation camp.

We really enjoyed the tawara stage. All through this stage the senior men watched over us and were teaching us.

We also danced, and they were teaching us all about that too. They were great teachers for we youngsters.

Wati nganmanyitja tjutangku, tawararitja tjuta atunymankunytja, tawaritja kulunypa tjuta. Atunymankunytja munu anga-wangka munu angapailta.

When young men are newly initiated, they remain in the segregated tawaritja camp, and are looked after there. They are overseen and spoken about in a roundabout way, and are still very much restricted in what they can do.

Ka tjana tawarangka nyinapai. Pukulpa, tawaritja tjuta. Pala palula tjana, kukaku ankupai maluku munuya malu paulpai munuya ngalya katipai tawarakutu munu tjana wati tjilpi tjuta ungkupai like tjamu or kuta, ngunytjuku, mamaku. Tjana kuka ngalya katipai. Ka nyara paluru, nyara paluru ara wiru, iriti ngarangi. Ka ara nyangatja tjinguru mawiyawiyaringanyi, wiyaringu.

They live in a tawara camp. They enjoy it very much, being amongst all the other tawara. But their task is to go hunting for kangaroo, cook it correctly, and bring it back for other tawara and the men, such as their senior grandfathers, and their older brothers, as well as their mothers and fathers. Their job is to bring plenty of meat back home. This is a wonderful part of our culture, which has been the tradition since ancient days. Sadly this tradition is slowly and gradually fading away.

Wati tawaritja kulunypa tjuta patu nyinanytjaku. Tawarangka kaya ngunytju mama, tjana pukulpa nyinapai panya katja, katja tjanampa tawarangka, kuta tjutaku kanyilpai, kuta pulka tjutangku, wati nganmanyitja tjutangku ka paluru tjana angakanyilpai.

Wati tawaritja (segregated, newly-initiated men) must remain living at a distance from everyone else. This is a feature of what makes a tawaritja camp what it is. The mothers and fathers are always so proud of their tawara sons when they are in the tawara camp, also knowing their older sons are there, caring for them. The role of the older brother is to teach their younger brothers when they are newly initiated and living in the tawara camp. Their role is to ensure the young men remain hidden and distant.

Tawaranguru, putu ananyi, minyma tjuta kutu, kami tjuta kutu, kungka tjuta kutu. Tawarangka tjana mauntalpa nyinapai. Munu paluru tjana rawa pukulpa nyinapai kukaku ankupai, kuta tjutangku katipai, kanyalaku apu kutu, kutjupara maluku katipai.

During the tawara camp, they are not allowed to go near any women, not their grandmothers or any other female. Tawara men must remain fully segregated. They must keep their focus on staying happy there, and concentrate solely on hunting with their older brothers, up into the mountains to hunt for hills kangaroos, or otherwise for plains kangaroos.

Munuya pitjapai, munu panya kuta tjutaku paluru tjana inma panya ngalypa-ngalypa, kantulpai mungaringkula (Nyii-nyii matuku piri) Tjala nya munu Wilypinpaku. Inma Wilypinpa, ayiniayini tjuta pakalpai tjana, pakara pakara paluru tjana pukulpa ngaripai. Kaya ngura kutjupa-kutjupa tjutaku pitjapai, nyakunytjikitja – palu minyma tjuta wiya.

When they come back to camp they can relax and enjoy playful singing and dancing with their older brothers, dancing into the night. They'll dance Zebra Finch dances (Nyii-nyii matuku piri) or say, Tjala (Honey Ants) or Inma Wiilypinpa (Eagles), all of which are lots of fun for them. They'll dance all night and then sleep well after a night of fun. Then they'll travel to many places, to have a look at the sites and to go hunting – but never in the company of women.

Ka alatji ngarangi pukulpa, like Fregon-ta, Anapalala, munu Amatala. Anangu tjutaku nyanga palunya kanyini aranya palunya. Strong, wituwitu, wiru. Tjukurpa tawaritjatjara wiyaringu, palu ngayulu nyiringka tjunanyi, tjana kulintjaku, 'Ai, tawaritja kunyu wirunya, wati tawaritja kulunypa tjuta, mauntalpa nyinanytja.'

That is how we always conducted our lives in Fregon, Ernabella and Amata. This is a long-lasting Anangu cultural tradition, and it is strong and important, with unbending rules.

> **The time-honoured standard of the tawara camp is beginning to fade but as I write about tawara I am reminded, 'Hey, the tawara tradition is so good, it just couldn't be a better way to train up our young men, segregated.'**

Ka Tjukurpa nyanga paluru manta nganampangka ngaranyi. Tjana wangkapaiya, ngura kutjupa kutu ankula, nyura patanma, ka anangungku, nguraritjangku kutju ankula kapi mantjini, munu ngalya katira unganyi, tii tjikintjaku. Or mingkulpa unganyi. Anyway, ankunytja wiya.

These stages of life on our country are part of our Tjukurpa Law. They would tell us that if we are ever travelling around, we must wait at certain locations for the traditional owners of the site to enter first, to be the one to get the water and bring it back, so we can make a cup of tea to drink. Or they may bring out wild tobacco. Either way, we are not at liberty to just go mindlessly in, any time we like.

Tjilpi yangapala tjukutjuku nyinanyangka. 'Palya, nyura pitja ngura kutu. Kami tjutaku, tjamu tjutaku.' Ka ngayulu patu nyinangi.

The senior old men always accompany the young men. 'Okay, you can all return home now. Go back to our grandmothers and grandfathers now.' I too had been camping a long way away.

Irkapiri nyinanyangka, Anitji tjana wangkapai.

In the irkapiri support camp, my family members were speaking the ceremonial language of Anitji.

Ngayunya katipai ngura pul̲ka kutu. Ngura pul̲ka, area miil̲miil̲pa. Ngayuku mamangku pailpai, 'Don't war̲u tilinma. Ila ankunytja wiya.' Ka war̲u tililpai, kapi tjutilpai, wati tjilpi tjut̲a. Ka nganan̲a ngurangka nyinapai.

I was taken to see sites of great significance, important places, sacred areas. We would only ever camp on our own country. My father warned me, 'Don't light fires here. Never allow them to come too close.' If a fire burns here, it must be put out with water by senior men.

Kampapai wiya. At̲unymankupai. Tjukul̲a at̲unymankupai. Tjana ankula kapi katira ungkupai. Palu put̲u ananyi anyway. Ngararitjangku kutju unganyi. Palula ngur̲u nganan̲a ngayulu nintiringkula kulinu. Uti ngayulu tjukurpa tjunama. Nganampa tjukurpa. Ngura pul̲ka.

Never burn this country. Take the greatest of care. Protect the rockholes. Only the traditional owners can enter these places, and bring water out to give to others. Nobody is allowed to just enter at random. Only the traditional landholders have the authority to give water from these places. I learnt the rules of the land from these teachings.

It was because of my traditional education that I decided to write it all down. Our Tjukurpa. Our sacred lands.

Kutjupara Yanyilu tjana ingkangi *Land Rights Act* tjara panya, 'Ngura miil̲miil̲pa tjara, tjukurpa alatjit̲u.' Ngayulu wangkapai, pipangka tjunu: 'Tjukurpa nganampa upa wiya, pul̲ka. Tjitji mal̲atja mal̲atja tjut̲aku. Tjana ngapartji take over-aringkunytjaku.' Palula nguru ngayulu walkatjunanyi.

Many years ago, Yanyi Bandicha sang and spoke the words to the *Land Rights Act* song,

'Ngura miil̲miil̲pa tjara, Tjukurpa alatjit̲u – it is the sacred ground of the Dreamtime.'

This is what I am saying too, and the message I have been putting in my paintings: 'Our Tjukurpa is not weak, it is powerful. It will be there for future generations of our children. Our descendants will take over from us.' This is why I keep painting this same message.

The words 'Kulilaya manta milmilpatjara Tjukurpa alatjitu' in Mumu Mike's *Postbag Painting* (2016) are lyrics from the first verse of 'Kulilaya (Listen, All of You)' – the Land Rights song. The first verse was written by Bill Davis and the song was recorded by him in 1980 with four women led by Sandra Ken. 'Kulilaya' was then first sung publicly during the protest march and rally in Victoria Square, Adelaide, on 14 February 1980, in support of Pitjantjatjara land rights.

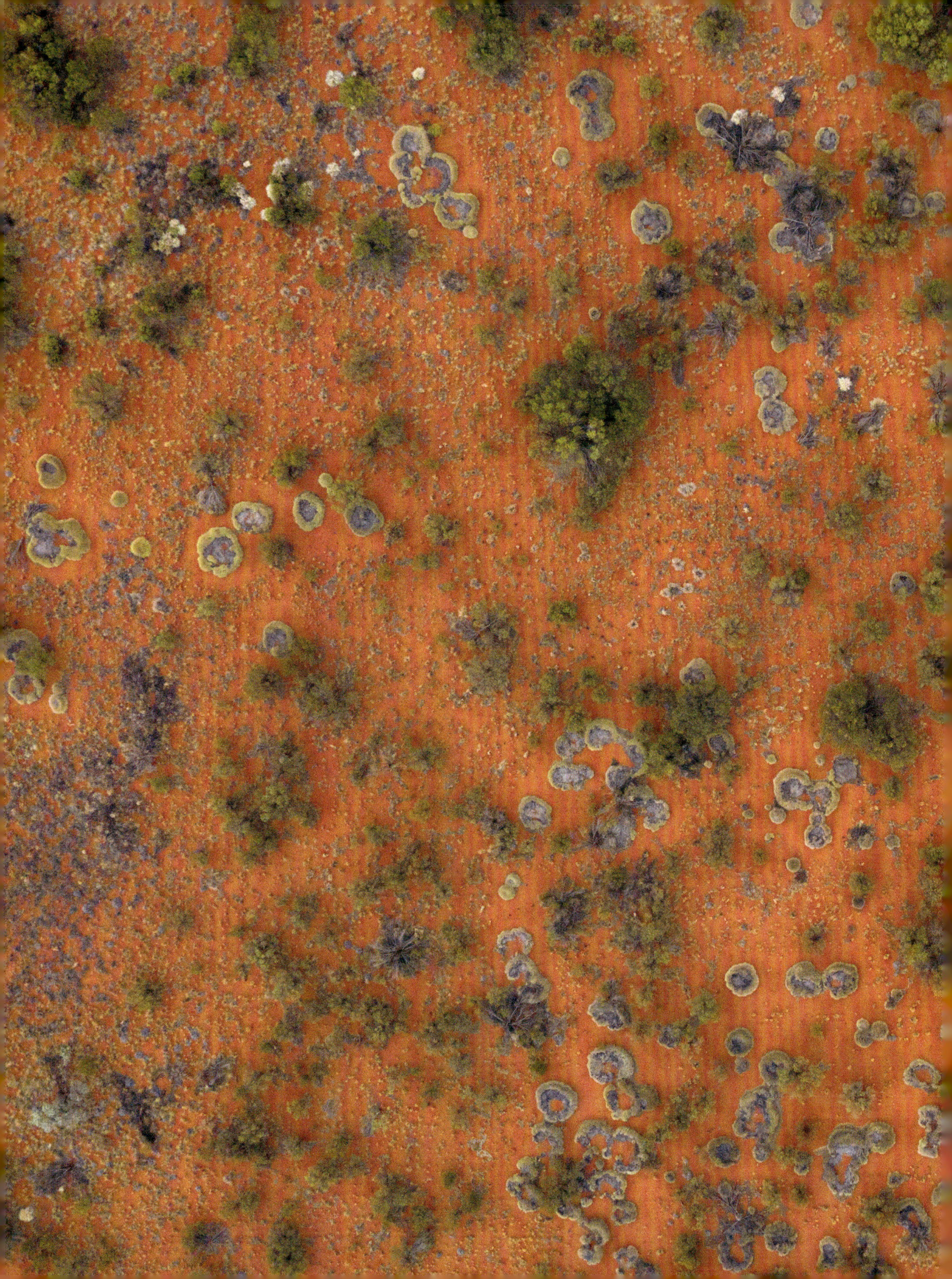

Nganampa Tjukurpa

Our Tjukurpa

Tjukurpa palunya, painting malatja ngayulu walkatjunu, kutju, pipa kutjupangka. Walkatjunu ngayulu, wati kutjungku. Wati malikitja. Kutjuku Australiala iriti tjunu, wangka kutjupa Australia manta nyangatja ultu, empty, *terra nullius*. Palu paluru ngunti wangkangu. Ngana<u>n</u>a tjuta tjara tjukurpa pulka tjara. Paluru ngunti wangkangi. Nganana tjukurpa pulka kanyini. Ngayulu wangkapai.

The Tjukurpa I was taught is the same message I keep putting in my paintings now. It is the same message, in different paintings. I am also writing my response to something one man once said. A man who was a stranger to this land. Many years ago, this man stated that Australia was an empty land, *terra nullius*. What he said was wrong. We are many people, with an enduring and powerful culture. What he said is simply not true. We people are rich in our own cultural heritage. I keep saying the same thing.

Uwa. Nganana, anangu tjutangku, Tjukurpa nganampa, manta nyangangka ngarantja. Nganana wati, munu nganana alatji. Munu nganana uparingayi. Like upa – weak nyinanyi. Tjukurpa nyinantja. Munu nganana tjukurpangka ngarala, nganampa kulintjaku. Miri nganampa kunpu ngarantjaku because pulka nyangatja nganampa ngaranyi.

We Anangu know the Tjukurpa on our land. The Tjukurpa is always there. Where there are key Tjukurpa sites, we are reminded of the stories. Our ancestors were strong people because they lived within the reality of Tjukurpa Law.

Page 30: Pila (spinifex plain) in Pitjantjatjara country.
Photo: Rohan Thomson, 2018

Munu Tjukurpa nganampa ngar̲anyi tjukul̲a tjut̲ala panya. Rockhole. Palu rockhole nyara palula, rockhole nyara palur̲u ini, initjara. Ka tjitji tjut̲angku ngurkantankunytjaku ngar̲anyi, 'Uwa ini nyangatja palur̲u, tjukul̲a nyangatja munu tjukuritja.'

Tjukurpa lies within every rockhole water source. Tjukul̲a, or rockholes. Each rockhole is known to us, and every rockhole has a name. They are all named places. Our children know and recognise each rockhole, 'Oh yes I know this rockhole. I know its name and the story associated with it.'

Kutjupar̲a Tjukurpa nganampa ngar̲anyi karungka. Tjukitja tjawal̲pai. Ka an̲angu tjut̲angku ngurkantjaku ngar̲anyi munu tjukitji nyangatja, kapitjara. Karu nyangatja. Karu ini nyangatja. Ka nyanga palunya, nganan̲a ini tjut̲a tjun̲a-tjun̲anyi. Rockhole. Karungka. Tjintjir̲a. Apu. Kapi tjara tjut̲a. Ka nyanga tjana ini tjara ngar̲anyi palya. An̲angungku ngurkantjaku. Munu kulini, 'Wai! Ngura ini nyangatja nyanga ila ngar̲anyi, ar̲a nganan̲a kapi kutu. Munu nganan̲a ananyi kapi kutu.

Other places of ours that have Tjukurpa are watercourses, creeks and riverbeds, known as karu. Within these systems are key water-holding soakage areas underneath the sand. This is a karu. Each karu has a name. Each named soakage area is dug to access the water. There can be rockholes in riverbeds too. Claypan. Mountainside. Water can be found in many places. Each water source is named and known. An̲angu recognise and know each water source. They think, 'Oh yes! Here we are, we are close to such and such a place, with such and such story at this water source. Let's go now to get some water.'

Munu nganan̲a kapi tjarangka wirkankupai munu nganan̲a rockhole-ngka ngaripai munu war̲u tjukutjuku tililpai. Mal̲u tjut̲a, mal̲u, kipar̲a, kal̲aya tjut̲a ngula ukir̲i pakanyangka pitjantjaku. Tjana pitjapai, ngurakutu tjana kul̲u ninti, ngura tjanampa palumpa, kapiku. Ka alatji Tjukurpa nyanga nganampa pul̲ka ngar̲anyi.

Overleaf: An̲angu walking towards the tjukul̲a (rockholes) at Victory Well, close to Mimili.
Photo: Rohan Thomson, 2018

When we arrive near to a water source, we might camp nearby for the night, and we will light a small management fire. Kangaroos, bush turkeys and emus will come along later to eat the fresh green vegetation that regenerates after fire. They'll be coming along to the water sources that they are familiar with, because the water sources are theirs too, they need water too. This is an example of our Tjukurpa governing behaviours.

Palu kutjupaṟa, wati tjuṯangku pailpai. Apu nyanga kutu ankunytja wiyangku wantima, manta miiḻmiiḻpa. Ka nganaṉa nguḻuringkupai. Bushfire palyalpai wiya. Waṟu tililpai wiya.

At other key sites, senior men may prohibit entry. The rocky hills thereabouts may be too sacred, and entry may be permanently forbidden. We respectfully avoid these places. Bushfires are forbidden. No fires are lit nearby.

Ngayulu panya nintiringu wati tjilpi tjuṯangku, tjamu tjuṯangku, kuṯa tjuṯangku. Munu ngayulu nintiringangi kapi tjuṯaku kuḻu. Munu pampa tjuṯa, kami tjuṯangku wangkapai. Munu inmangka kuḻu. Inmangkaya nganaṉanya aḻtipai. Nyinantjaku, tjitjiku.

The senior old men taught these rules, as did my grandfathers and older brothers. They taught me the regulations governing water sources. The senior old women and my grandmothers also taught me the Law. Law can be expressed by song too. We can be called to order by song. Children come and sit down to learn.

Ka nyara palula aṟa nganampa. Tjukurpa nganampa manta nganampangka. Tjukurpa puḻka ngaṟanyi. Tjukurpa tjuṯa – tjamu tjuṯangku ungkupai. 'Nyangatja nyuntumpa tjamuku ngura.' Ka kamingku wangkapai, 'Nyangatja nyuntumpa kamiku ngura. Munu kuṉpu ngaṟama munu aṯunytjunama.' Ka alatji nganaṉa kuṉpu tjunanyi.

These are examples of our traditional ways. Our Tjukurpa governing the laws of our land. Tjukurpa with great strength and power. Tjukurpa of great diversity, that has been handed down through the ages by our grandfathers. 'This is your grandfathers' country.' Our grandmothers say, 'This is your grandmothers' country. Keep it strong and keep safeguards in place.' We have ways of protecting and keeping our land safe.

Piranpa tjutangku ngurpa. Kutjupa tjuta ninti. Pitjalaya nintiringu munu tjana kulinu. Walypala kutjupa tjutangku ninti, tjukurpa tjanampa ngaranyi. Ka ara nyanga paluru, Tjukurpa nganampangka ngaranyi. Watarku tjarpantja wiya.

White people are mostly unaware of our cultural rules. Having said that, some do know. Some white people come to our lands and they learn quickly. Some white people understand cultural rules, because they observe their own cultural traditions. We too have cultural traditions and laws, called Tjukurpa. Don't come to our land unaware of this.

Kutjupara nganana palya pitjapai munu nguraritja tjutangku waru tililpai, 'Kapiku nyura palya ara!' Ka tjana kapi tjutilpai, or nguraritjangku malu katipai, munu ungkupai. Ka tjana pukulpa paltja nyinapai. Watarku ankunytja wiya.

Occasionally we are welcomed to a place while the traditional owners are lighting management fires, 'You are welcome to go to the water!' They'll pour some water for us, or the traditional owners might bring kangaroo meat, and give us some. They enjoy sharing their food. So be mindful when entering their lands.

Like nyangatja tjinguru, kutjupangku tjinguru, 'Ai, manta nyangatja wiru! Palu ultu!' Palu ngunti wangkanyi. Manta nyangangka tjuta ngaranyi. Anangu tjuta. Tjukurpa tjuta. Tjukuritja tjuta. Nyara paluru ngaranyi. Ka nganana Tjukurpa nyanga paluru tjananya kanyira, nganana kunpu ngaranyi.

Overleaf: Kakalyalya (Major Mitchell's cockatoos) around Victory Well.
Photo: Rohan Thomson, 2018

Let's say, someone might exclaim, 'Hey, this is a beautiful place! Yet this is an empty land!' But they are wrong. This land is rich and full. Full of Anangu. Full of Tjukurpa. Full of ancestral spirit. It is all here. We are each responsible for our own Tjukurpa, but are collectively strong.

Tjana tjinguru ankupai ngura miilmiilpa-kutu, nguraritja mulapa kutju. Munu tjana ngura patu tjunkupai munu tjana tjitji pailpai, 'Waru tilintja wiya! Ankunytja wiya!' Ka wati tjilpi tjutangku kutju, nguraritja tjutangku kapi mantjilpai. Munu nyaratja paltjalpai, ungkupai.

People in charge regularly visit their sacred sites, but only the absolute traditional owners. They maintain the regulations over the distant places and remind children, 'Do not set fire to the bush! Stay away from that place!'

Kutjuparaya mirapai munu aalpiringku wangkapai. Early bird pakara wangkapai. 'Kutju para ngarantja wiya! Ngura patu kutu ankunytja wiya! Ngurangka nyinama!' Tjinguru watingku punkuku. Wakalku. Kulypalpa tjutangku putu paini. Kuta tjutangku kutju.

On occasion people may be shouted at, or sternly addressed during aalpiri public speeches. Early birds wake up and begin the aalpiri speeches. 'Don't go bush by yourself! Don't go wandering off to distant places! Stay near home!' This is because men are out hunting with spears, and could kill people. Spear them to death. One's uncle cannot give commands like that. Only the older brother can.

Ka Tjukurpa nyanga paluru, change-iringkunytja wiya. Still ngaranyi, wirunya.

These cultural rules have not changed. They are still in operation, I'm glad to say.

Manta nyangaku Tjukurpa kunpu. Nyara palula ngananа wangkanyi. Manta nyangaku Tjukurpa kunpu. Tjitji malatja malatja nintiringkula kunpu kanyintjaku. Paluru ngayulu tjunkunytjikitja mukuringanyi.

The Tjukurpa Law of the land is still strong here. We still talk like this. The Tjukurpa of the land remains strong and true. We want our future descendants to learn to be strong children. It is for them that I want to write my story.

Tjukurpa nganampa pulka ngaranyi atunymankunytjaku ngura miilmiilpa, miilmiilpa tjuta, munu tjitji tjuta nintintjaku. Ngura miilmiilpangka itingka waru tilintja wiya, wantintjaku. Tjukurpa nganampa kunpu. Nguraritjangku kutju ngura kanyilpai, munu Tjukurpa.

Our Law is the authority we draw on to actively protect our sacred sites, our numerous sites of significance, and to teach the younger generation to never allow fires to burn near any sacred site. Our Law is potent and strong. The traditional owners are responsible for their land and their Tjukurpa.

Tjinguru piranpa kutju pitjanyi – paluru ngurpa – paluru ngunti walytjaringanyi, munu nganampa ngura – nganampa Tjukurpa upani.

Let's say a white person arrives on our land – they are ignorant of our Law, and yet they claim a kinship to us and our land – thus diminishing the value of our Tjukurpa Law.

Palu wati malikitja pitjala nguraritja tjutangka tjapini – wati tjilpi tjutangka munu minyma pampa tjutangka – tjapilpai, 'Ngayulu palya ngura nyangangka wirkaku?' Panya nguraritja tjuta, paluru tjana key kanyini, munu alani. Anangu tjuta tjarpara anangu malikitja tjarpara munu nintiringanyi. Palumpa way wiya – paluru tjana nguraritjaku way. Munu ngura ngurkantankunytjaku.

But if a strange man comes to us and asks the traditional owners – the senior elder men and the senior elder women – asks, 'Is it acceptable for me to enter your land?' If he asks the right traditional owners, then they are the ones who hold the key, and the right to open the way to visitors and strangers, to enter and to receive intelligence. The way in is not that man's right – it is the way in as determined by the traditional owners. They know the natural, cultural and social values of the site.

Kultukata wiya. You can’t go kultukata. You gotta go tjukaruru.

You can’t take a short cut with this. You must not take any short cuts. You must take the straight and narrow path according to the Law.

Ngurarítja tjuta kutju, wati tjilpiku ngura kutjupa tjuta kutu sellamilantja wiya. Kuntangka. Palya wiya nyangatja. Tjukurpa nganampa titutjara ngaranyi. Malatja malatja tjutaku. Tjitji tjutaku. Kungka tjutaku.

> **None of we traditional owners of this land are authorised to sell any part of our land. What a shameful thought. It would be unthinkable. Sacred power is eternally potent in the landscape. It will be the inheritance of children of the future. All our children, all the girls.**

Ka ara irititja nganampa tjukurpa wiyaringkunytja wiya. Ngaranyi. Ngana<u>n</u>a piruku utinytjaku, you know, like, nyaa purunypa, like Aliwanyuwanyu-nya ka ngana<u>n</u>a nyangu, ‘Ai, mina wiya.’ Palu nintiku tjana, iriti, ‘Tjawala!’ Ka tjawara mina ngalya pakalpai, ka tjanampa nyiinyii, tjanpi nyiinyii tjunkupai ka mina palula nguru wirunya, clear pakalpai.

Much of our traditional lifestyle has not disappeared. It remains strong. There are so many important skills we continue to impart, you know, for instance, like, say, at Aliwanyuwanyu waterhole. If we see it and someone says, ‘Oh, it’s empty,’ someone with the old knowledge will say, ‘Well, dig down then!’ If we dig into a waterhole, water will rise into the hole, and if we place a filter pad of nyiinyii grass on the surface, it will make the water crystal clear.

Ka Tjukurpa nganampa wiyaringkunytja wiya. Ngana<u>n</u>a ara nyara palunya utinytjaku, yangupala tjuta alpamilantjaku, you know, ara nganampangka kulintjaku.

Our Tjukurpa Law is not ending. We convey our Law messages to our young men to help them along in life, you know, so that they always have the old knowledge around them.

Kulilaya munuya nitiriwa
Listen to us, and learn from us

Panya ngayulu nyanganyi tjitjingku iriti like nganampa tjamu tjuta munu Pitjantjatjara tjuta wati tjilpi tjuta munu Yankunytjatjara panya paluru tjana tjukurpa kutjungka nyinanyi. Tjuta tjara wiya.

Many years ago, when I was still a little boy, I used to observe my grandfather and all the other senior and wise old Pitjantjatjara and Yankunytjatjara men living by the one Law. Not according to any individual whim.

Munuya pukulpa nyinanyi munuya manta atunymanangi, tjanampa, munu tjana ankupai tjanampa ngura kutu. Munuya tjitji tjuta katipai munu-ya nintilpai, tjanampa ngura tjana ngula atunymankunytjaku ngura palumpa tjanampa.

They were content and fulfilled in their lives, managing their country, living on their own land. They always took the young children around the land, teaching them everything about it, so they in turn would care and protect it.

Ka panya tjana iriti tjilpi munu pampa tjuta paluru tjana kunpu ngaranyi. Kunpu ngarangi munu paluru tjana pukulpa nyinangi. Pukulpa nyinangi munuya atunymankupai, ka rawa nguwanpa nyinara ngayulu nyiinkaringu, munu watiringu.

Back then, the wise old men and the wise old women were dynamic and strong. They were vigorous and healthy too. They were vigorous in their caring for their country, and I observed this all through my childhood, youth and early manhood.

Munu ngayulu nyangu tilpi tjutangkuya mantjinu manta, panya kapmantangku tjananya ungu Itjinpirila. Ka ngali yangapalangku nyinangi nyara palunya. Ka tjananya ungu, one side wiya, palu kapmanta paluru pitjangu, ka tjilpi tjutangku katingu puti kutu munu nintinu.

I witnessed the senior old people win back the rights to their own land, which was returned ceremonially by the government, at Itjinpiri. We young men watched it all unfolding. We saw how the government gave back the land to its rightful owners after being taken out into the bush country by the old men and shown places.

Ka kapmanta nintiringu munu kulinu, 'Ai, mulapa, tjanampa tjukararu ngaranyi.' Munu tjananya kalkunu unkunytjikitjangku Land Rights Act. Munu ungu palu paluru wangkangu, 'Kulinma, walawurungku purunypa nyanganyi, katu nguru nyanganyi tjulyantjaku tawara.'

Once the government had seen and learnt certain facts, they realised then, 'Hey, this mob are speaking the truth.' That's when they made the promise that they would return the land in the form of a Land Rights Act. They did this, saying, 'Listen, this will protect you like an eagle flies high above the land, seeing all, ensuring it is not stolen from you.'

Ka palula nguru ngayulu tjukurpa ngayuku walkatjunanyi painting-ngka, ngura winkingku nyakunytjaku munu kulintjaku, 'Munta mulapa tjanampa ara munu wangka munu ngura.' Ngananna nganampa wangka wiya ngarinyangka ngananna wiya, weak, ngura nganampa wiya ngaranyangka ngananna putu kulini, palu ngura nganampa pulka, tjukurpa pulka.

For all these reasons and more I have been documenting my cultural life in paintings, so that people everywhere can see them and hopefully come to realise, 'Oh we see, now we understand a bit more about their lives and history, their language and their homes.' Our language is not dead; we are not weak people, we are not without land and we are not without culture; on the contrary, our culture is incredibly strong.

Manta nganampa nyaa tjukurtjara. Tjukurpa tjara.

Our land is filled with deep cultural heritage and Law. This is our Tjukurpa.

Kulilaya munuya nitiriwa Australia, palya? Wa<u>l</u>awurungku rawangku nyanganyi manta Tjukurpa kutitjunkunytjikitjangku. Wati tjilpi ngurariṯjangku a<u>t</u>unymankupai Tjukurpa munu manta. Manta munu Tjukurpa ti<u>t</u>utjara nga<u>r</u>anyi. A<u>l</u>ariwa pina. Ngunti walytjararingkula Tjukurpa munu manta kurantja wiya.

Listen to us, and learn from us Australia, okay? Eagles watch over our land and anyone wanting to steal our cultural heritage. Our senior men are safeguarding the traditional lands and cultural heritage in the same way. Our land and Tjukurpa.

Overleaf: *Kulilaya munuya nitiriwa (Listen and learn from us)*, 2017
Mumu Mike Williams, Sammy Dodd (spears)
synthetic polymer paint and ink on canvas mailbags, with ku<u>l</u>a<u>t</u>a (spears) made from ku<u>l</u>a<u>t</u>a (spearbush), mulga, ma<u>l</u>u pulyku (kangaroo tendon) and ki<u>t</u>i (mulga leaf resin)
220 x 250 cm
Arthur Roe Collection
Photo: Merinda Campbell, Museum and Art Gallery of the Northern Territory
Finalist for the 35th Telstra National Aboriginal & Torres Strait Islander Art Awards

Kulilaya Munuya
Nitiriwa
AUSTRALIA
PALYA?
No.1
Munta
IS A CRIMINAL OFFENCE
PENALTIES APPLY
ALariWA PiNA

AUSTRALIA
02-11
MANTA
munu
TjuKurpA
Titutjara
ngaranyi
Tjukurpa
FT OR MISUSE OF THIS BAG
S A CRIMINAL OFFENCE
PENALTIES APPLY
A TjuKurpA
WiyA

Canvas munu kuḻaṯa

Canvas and spears

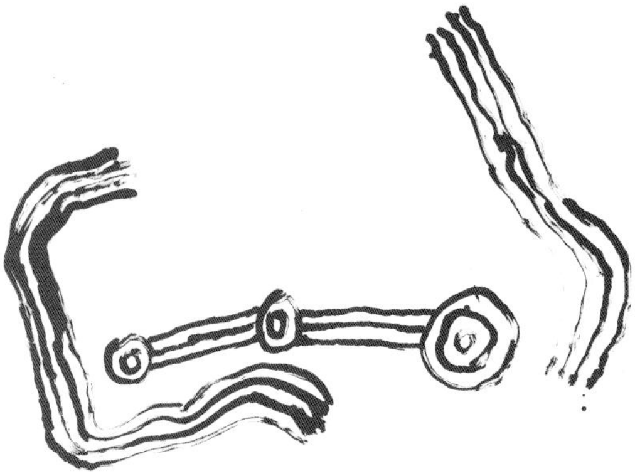

Uwa, ngayulu iriti nguru Tjukurpa Minyma Kutjara paintamilaningi, Tjukurpa Minyma Kutjara ankunytja. Paluru pula ngura parari nguru pakara anu, Pukatjala nguru, munu Kelvins Well-ta wanu pitjangu, Palm Valley munu Camel Farm-ta wanu ma pitjangu Telegraph Station-ta kutu. Minyma Kutjara ngayulu nyaa walkatjunu, C shapes panya.

I've been painting for a long time now, always painting my Tjukurpa, Minyma Kutjara (Two Women), about two sisters travelling on country. They travelled a long way, starting out in my country, near Pukatja on the APY Lands, and then the sisters travelled through places that are now called Kelvins Well, Palm Valley and Camel Farm on their way to Telegraph Station. The Minyma Kutjara are the C-shapes in my paintings.

Kuwari, year nyangatja 2016 ngayulu tjatamilanu nyaa paintamilaningi, map panya, Australiala winki tjara, ara tjakultjunkunytjaku. Ka ngayulu tjukurpa Pitjantjatjara walkatjunkupai kutju, tjukurpa nyaa tjara, tjilpi pampa tjutangku ngura palula titutjara kanyini, ngura miilmiilpa tjuta, malatja malatja tjutaku. Ngayulu wangkapai tjukurpa wiru tjuta, nganampa tjukurpa kunpu kanyinytjikitjangku. Australia map panya tjukurpa uwankaraku, Ananguku munu piranpa tjutaku, Australiala winki.

I started painting the map of Australia in 2016 and using my paintings to talk about important things. I write in Pitjantjatjara about how the old men and women are custodians of their land, how they've got to keep culture strong, protect sacred sites and pass all their knowledge on to the younger ones. I'm talking about things where I live, about how we've got to be strong and protect our land and culture. The map of Australia shows that even though I'm writing in my language and talking about my country, these stories are important for Aboriginal people everywhere, all over Australia.

Tjukurpa nyaa nyangatja? Tjukurpa land rights tjara, nganampa *Land Rights Act*. Tjukurpa pulka mulapa. Tjukurpa mulapa, nganampa uwankaraku, Anangu tjutaku kutju. Ngayulu wangkapai, 'Nyaa manta? Land rights nyaa? Tjilpi pampa tjuta – tjana Tjukurpa wiru mulapa kanyini, tjanampa tjukurpa iriti nguru alatjitu. Tjilpi pampaku kutju, ngura nyangatja. Kulinma: manta munu Tjukurpa kunpungku kanyinma! Atunymanama, munu titutjara kanyinma, Anangu uwankaraku munu malatja malatja tjutaku.'

With my paintings I'm talking about land rights, and what the *Land Rights Act* means for Anangu. It's really important for us. I'm saying,

'Nyaa manta? What is land rights? All the old men and women here on these lands – they're the owners of the Tjukurpa, their Law and culture, their heritage. This land belongs to the old men and women. Listen: keep the land and its stories strong! Protect it and keep it strong for us – for everybody.'

Painting nyangatja, frame panya, Sammy Doddtu palyanu, wati Mimilila ngurara. Sammylu kulata wiru tjuta palyalpai, kulata irititja purunypa; punu tjara, kiti tjara munu malu pulyku tjara. Sammynya ngali wangkara kulilpai tjukurpa kulataku, munuli painting wiru tjuta palyalpai, tjukurpa pulka tjara. Kulata tjuta tjukurpa kunpu kanyini, ngaṉana ngura nganampa atunymankupai, kulatangka. Sammynya ngali yangapala iriti tjungu warkaringi station-ngka, munuli nyakukatira kulilpai *Land Rights Act*. Ka kuwari nganana uwankara uti kunpungku kanyinma munu kulinma, nganampa manta munu Tjukurpa.

The frames for my paintings are made by another senior man from Mimili, Sammy Dodd. Sammy still makes kulata the old way; using punu (wood), kiti (resin made from mulga tree leaf) and malu pulyku (kangaroo tendon).

Me and Sammy talked about using the kulata and the paintings together to send a strong message. Those spears show that we're protecting our land and culture – we're guarding it. Me and Sammy both worked on stations when we were young men, we've seen the changes because of the *Land Rights Act*. It's up to us now, all of us, to look after our land and keep our culture strong.

Overleaf: Sammy Dodd and Mumu Mike Williams in front of Sammy's truck, which he uses for land management and to collect materials for kuḻaṯa (spears), 2017.
Photo: Jackson Lee

DODGE
245

'I'm still making kuḻaṯa every day'
Sammy Dodd

When I was young I travelled everywhere, me and my old fella with his camel wagon: Indulkana, Ernabella, Kenmore, Granite Downs – we went everywhere, watching this mob and that mob, watching and seeing tjilpi tjuṯa (many old men) making kuḻaṯa (spear), miru (spear thrower) and kaḻi (boomerang). I learnt this way as a young man, sitting and watching, listening to the stories. Back then they made kuḻaṯa for hunting. Not anymore. Today, I've got my father's .22.

I haven't always made kuḻaṯa though. For a long time I was a cowboy, working on Everard Park Station near Mimili. After the cattle station finished and work stopped, we started making kuḻaṯa, kaḻi and miru. Wati tjuṯa tjungu (us men together). Not for hunting, not for selling. We just sat down, talked stories and made kuḻaṯa. We would talk a lot of Tjukurpa, but I can't say any more about those stories, wanti (leave it alone).

I'm still making kuḻaṯa every day. My teachers have passed on a long time ago and now I have become the teacher. The youngfellas sometimes rush me and rush the kuḻaṯa, but they will learn that it is not a quick process. Finding the right kuḻaṯa (spearbush) is first, cutting it out the right length. The kuḻaṯa bush is kaḻi-kaḻi puḻka (very bent), so making a fire and straightening the wood is very important: heat, bend, heat, bend, slowly making it straight.

There are many different ways of making kuḻaṯa. Not every kuḻaṯa needs a waṯa (spearhead) for example. I always make hunting kuḻaṯa with waṯa (head) and mukuḻpa (barb) from the mulga tree. Not too wide, not too long, sharpening and smoothing it for good throwing. The waṯa is attached with kiṯi (bush glue) and maḻu pulyku (kangaroo tendon). Kiṯi (bush glue) comes from a different kind of mulga (*Acacia minyura*), from the leaf. I dry the leaves for two days, then beat the dry resin out, then heat it and make a big batch of kiṯi, strong like a rock. I only use a little bit for each kuḻaṯa, so the kiṯi lasts a long time. To attach the waṯa, I heat kiṯi kuḻunypa (a little bit of bush glue) in the fire to make it soft. Then I tie it all together extra strong with ma<u>l</u>u pulyku (kangaroo tendon), which I first have to chew like chewing gum, softening it and pulling off long bits to bind the ki<u>t</u>i. This same way is used (ki<u>t</u>i and ma<u>l</u>u pulyku) to attach the muku<u>l</u>pa. You see, it's a long process. Today, the youngfellas learn the same way I did. Sitting and watching, listening to the stories, slowly.

Sammy Dodd making a ku<u>l</u>a<u>t</u>a (spear) at Mimili Maku Arts, 2018.

Nganampa manta Tjukurpa miilmiilpa tjuta tjara.
Pampuntja wiyangku wantima alatjitu!
Tjilpi munu pampa Tjukurpaku mayatja. Munu ninti pulka.
Ngintaka nganampa Tjukurpa. Piranpaku wiya munu government-ku wiya.
Palya?

Our land and Tjukurpa are sacred.
Don't touch them!
The old men and women are in charge of Tjukurpa. They're wise.
Ngintaka Tjukurpa is our story. It is not for whitefellas or government.
Okay?

Tjilpi munu pampangku Tjukurpa kunpu kanyintjaku (It's the senior men and senior women who keep the Law strong), 2016
Mumu Mike Williams, Sammy Dodd (spears)
ink and tea on paper, spears made from kulata (spearbush) and mulga, malu pulyku (kangaroo tendon) and kiti (mulga leaf resin)
150 x 100 cm
Collection of The University of Queensland, purchased 2016
Photo: Carl Warner

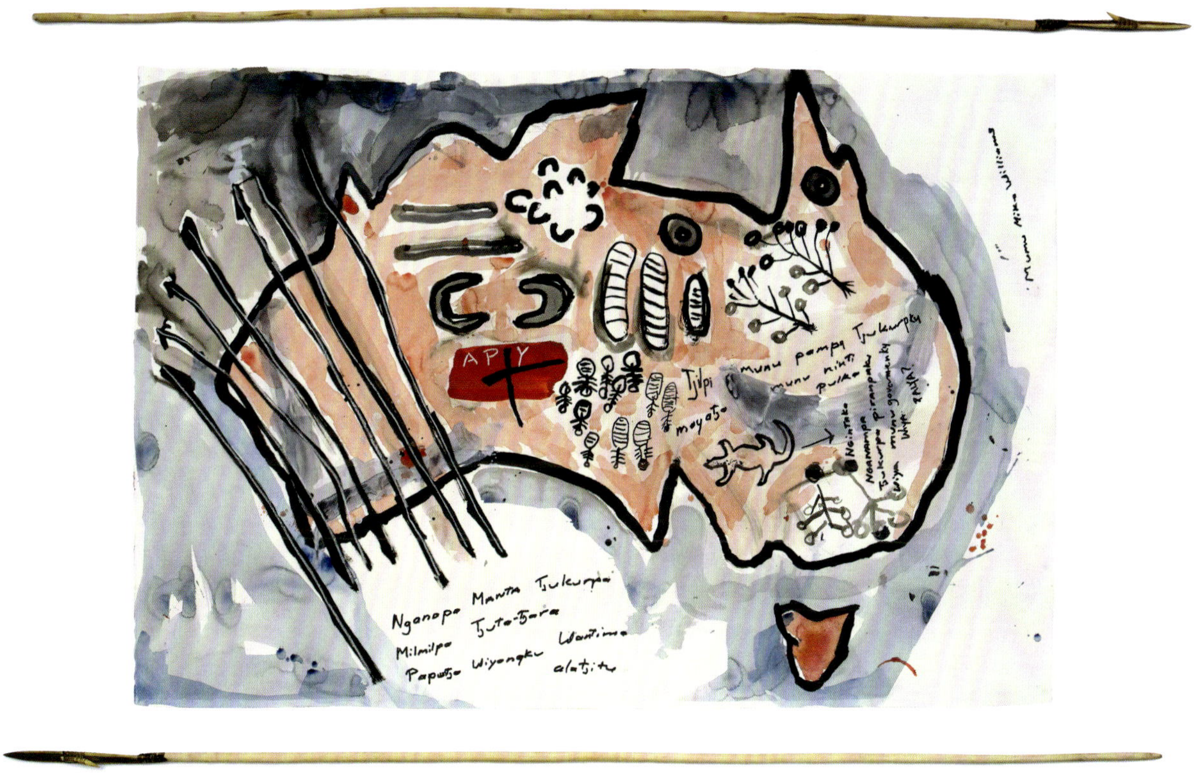
APY
Tjilpi
munu pampa Tjukurpa
munu ninti pulka
mayatja
Nganopa Manta Tjukurpa
Milmilpa Tjuta-Tjara
Papatja Wiyangku Wantima
alatjitu

Tjilpiku Pampaku
Anga kanyilpai
Tjanampa Tjukutjara
Kulilaya Manta Milmipa
Tjaka Tjukurpa Alatjitu
Kaya Papuntja Wiyangku
Wantima

Tjilpiku pampaku angakanyilpai tjanampa tjukurtjara.
Kulilaya. Manta miiḻmiiḻpa tjara tjukurpa alatjiṯu.
Kaya pampuntja wiyangku wantima.

The old men and women are guarding culture.
Listen. This is sacred land.
Don't touch it.

Tjilpi munu pampangku Tjukurpa kuṉpu kanyintjaku (It's the senior men and senior women who keep the Law strong), 2016
Mumu Mike Williams, Sammy Dodd (spears)
ink and tea on paper, spears made from kuḻaṯa (spearbush) and mulga, maḻu pulyku (kangaroo tendon) and kiṯi (mulga leaf resin)
150 x 100 cm
Collection of The University of Queensland, purchased 2016
Photo: Carl Warner

Kulilaya. Pampuntja wiya.
Tjilpi munu pampaku Tjukurpa kunpu kanyinytjaku.
Manta miilmiilpa tjara.

Listen. Don't touch.
The old men and women are the ones who are really protecting culture.
This is sacred land.

Tjilpi munu pampangku Tjukurpa kunpu kanyintjaku (It's the senior men and senior women who keep the Law strong), 2016
Mumu Mike Williams, Sammy Dodd (spears)
ink and tea on paper, spears made from kulata (spearbush) and mulga, malu pulyku (kangaroo tendon) and kiti (mulga leaf resin)
150 x 100 cm
Collection of The University of Queensland, purchased 2016
Photo: Carl Warner

KULILAYA
PAMPUNTJA
WIYA
TJILPI MUNU
PAMPAKU
TJUKURPA
KUNPU KANYINTJAKU
MANTA
MILMILPA TJARA
Mumu Mike Williams

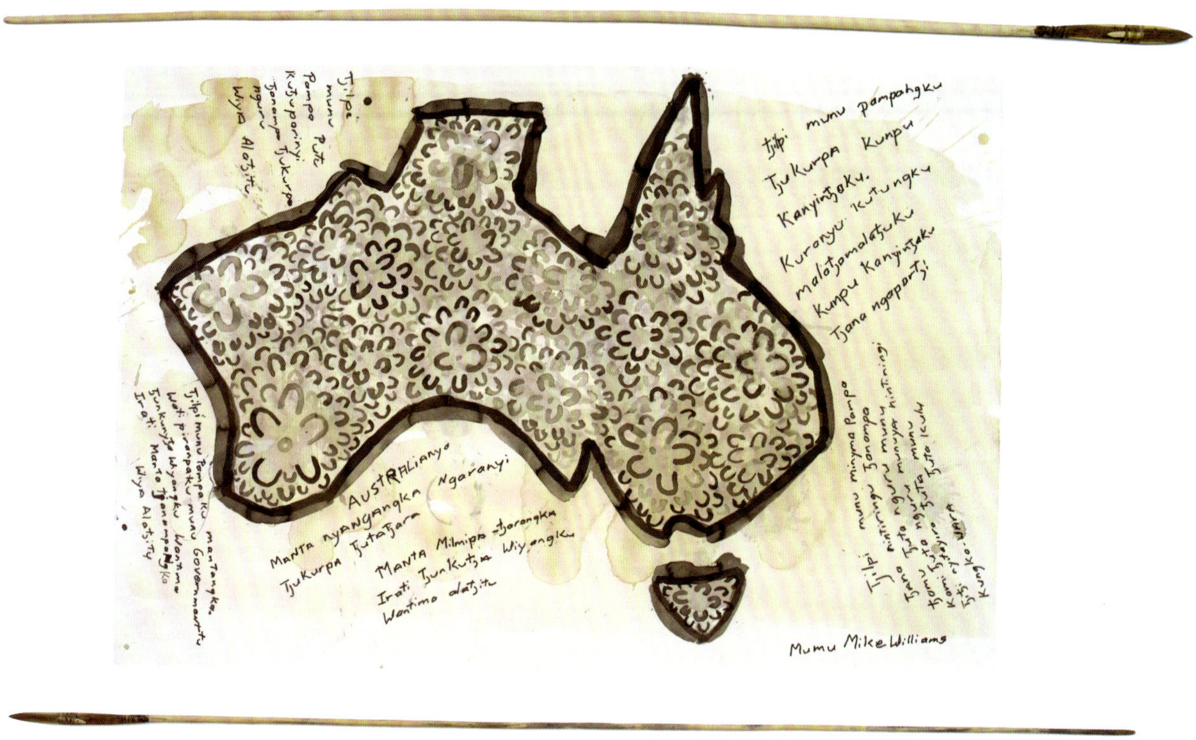
Tjilpi munu pampangku
Tjukurpa Kunpu
Kanyintjaku.
Kuranyu kutungku
malatjamalatjuku
Kunpu Kanyintjaku
Tjana ngaparitji
AUSTRALIanya
Manta nyanganka Ngaranyi
Tjukurpa Tjutatjara
Manta Milmipa tjarangka
Irati Tjunkutja Wiyangku
Wantima alatjitu
Mumu Mike Williams

Tjilpi munu pampa puṯu kutjuparinyi tjanampa Tjukurpa nguṟu.
Wiya alatjiṯu.
Tjilpi munu pampaku mantangka.
Wati piṟanpaku munu government-tu: Tjunkunytja wiyangku wantima iraṯi! Manta tjanampangka wiya alatjiṯu.
Australianya manta nyangangka ngaṟanyi Tjukurpa tjuṯa tjara.
Manta miiḻmiiḻpa tjarangka iraṯi tjunkunytja wiyangku wantima alatjiṯu.
Tjilpi munu pampaku Tjukurpa kuṉpu kanyinytjaku.
Kuranyu kutungku maḻatja maḻatjaku kuṉpu kanyinytjaku tjana ngapartji.
Tjilpi munu minyma pampa tjana nintiringu tjanampa tjamu tjuṯa nguṟu munu kami tjuṯa nguṟu, munuya nintiningi tjitji nyiṯayira tjuṯa munu kungkawaṟa tjuṯa kuḻu.

The old men and women never change from their Tjukurpa. Nothing changes.
The old men and women are responsible for the land.
Whitefellas and government: Don't put that poison here – we don't want it!
This is our inherited land.
Australia is a land rich in Tjukurpa.
Do not put poisonous nuclear waste dumps on our sacred land.
The old men and women want to keep their Tjukurpa alive.
They learnt the traditional ways from their ancestors, and now in turn, they are teaching the next generations.
The old men and the old women were taught by their grandparents, and they are now handing down the knowledge to the boys and girls and the next generations.

Tjilpi munu pampangku Tjukurpa kuṉpu kanyintjaku (It's the senior men and senior women who keep the Law strong), 2016
Mumu Mike Williams, Sammy Dodd (spears)
ink and tea on paper, spears made from kuḻaṯa (spearbush) and mulga, maḻu pulyku (kangaroo tendon) and kiṯi (mulga leaf resin)
150 x 100 cm
Collection of The University of Queensland, purchased 2016
Photo: Carl Warner

Kulilaya, Tjukurpa nyangatja Iyukutanyatjara mungaṯu wati piṟanpa tjuṯangku kuraṟa pungu mutukaku manta urinytjikitjangku. Kapamantangku, antjapalitjingku munu Umuwalu lankantjulangku nyangatja kurakura puḻka mulapa nguraritja kulintja wiyangku.

Listen, this Tjukurpa – Iyukuta [at the site of my birthplace, Inturtjanu] – was damaged some time ago by whitefellas taking rock to build a road. Government, anthropology and the land council at Umuwa never listened properly to the traditional owners.

Iyukuta Tjukurpa (detail), 2016
Mumu Mike Williams, Sammy Dodd (spears – not pictured)
tea, ink, acrylic and chalk pastel on 300 gsm watercolour paper, with kuḻaṯa (spear) frame made from kuḻaṯa (spearbush) and mulga, maḻu pulyku (kangaroo tendon) and kiṯi (mulga leaf resin)
150 x 100 cm
Artbank collection, purchased 2017

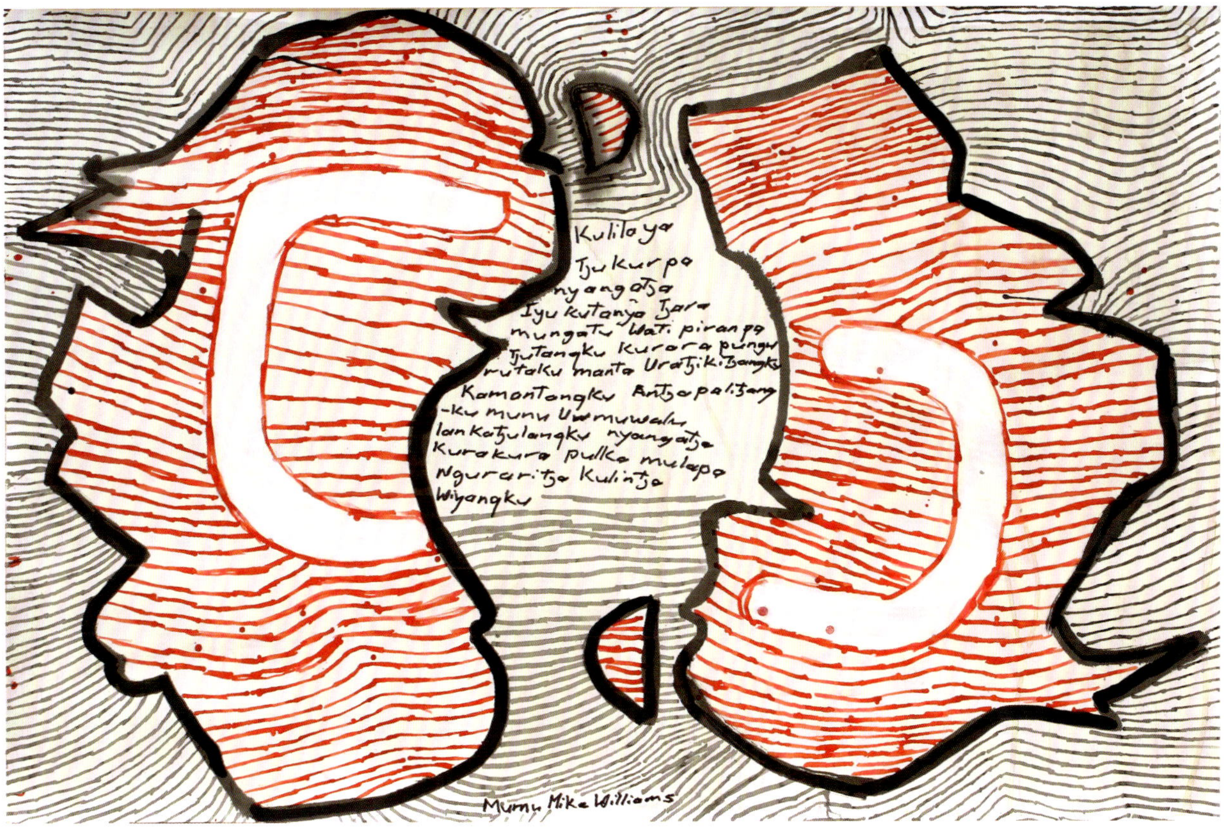
Kulilaya
Tjukurpa
nyangatja
Iyu kutanya Tjara
mungatu Wati piranpa
Tjutangku kurara pungu
rutaku manta Uratjikitjangku
Kamantangku Antjapalitjang
-ku munu Uwmuwalu
lankatjulangku nyangatja
Kurakura pulka mulapa
Ngurāritja Kulintja
Wiyangku
Mumu Mike Williams

Manta ngurira tjawara kurantja ngura miilmiilpa Tjukurpa winki.

Kunta wiya alatjitu.

Pina wiya kuru wiya.

Wati tjilpi mulapa tjuta munu minyma pampa tjuta tjana ngura miilmiilpa - anga kanyilpai.

Kurakura nganampa Tjukurpa kurarapungku manta tjawara rutaku pakara kamantangku pitjala anangu nguraritja wangka-wangkantja wiya.

Kunta wiya alatjitu.

Tjukuritja ngayuku katantananyi munu kurarapungu Tjukurpa Minyma Kutjara Iyukuta.

Kamantangku kurani kunta wiyangku.

Kulila, wati tjilpi munu minyma pampa ngarama kunpu panya Tjukurpa kunpu mulapa ngaranyi ngura miilmiilpa tjara kulu.

Kamanta pina pati kuru pati.

Wati tjilpi tjutangku wangkapai, 'Manta nganampa Tjukurpa nganampa ngura miilmiilpa tjuta nganampa ara. Nganampa wangka. Nganampa titutjara alatjitu malatja malatja tjutaku. Kulinma Tjukurpa.'

Page 70–1: *Kulinma Tjukurpa Kunpu Nyangatja,* 2016
Mumu Mike Williams, Sammy Dodd (spears)
tea, ink and oil pastel on 300 gsm watercolour paper, with kulata (spear) frame made from kulata (spearbush) and mulga, malu pulyku (kangaroo tendon) and kiti (mulga leaf resin)
150 x 150 cm
Finalist, National Works on Paper Prize 2018

Digging up the earth for mining damages our Tjukurpa, our land, and our sacred sites.
The mining companies, they've got no shame.
They've got no ears and no eyes.
The old men and women, the senior cultural elders, they look after the land, the heritage and the sacred sites – they don't want mining.
The government's road upgrades have made a mess of the land and they never asked the traditional owners' permission.
They've got no shame.
My sacred heritage site Tjukurpa Minyma Kutjara Iyukuta has been damaged and desecrated by the road upgrade.
The government is deaf and blind to this, they are not paying attention. They've got their eyes and ears closed.
The old men and women are standing up strong, they remember all the Tjukurpa, the strong stories, they're standing up strong, and they are saying,
'It's our land, our Tjukurpa, our sacred sites, our history, our heritage, our language, everything. We've got to look after it and keep it strong for the future generations. Listen to this important story.'

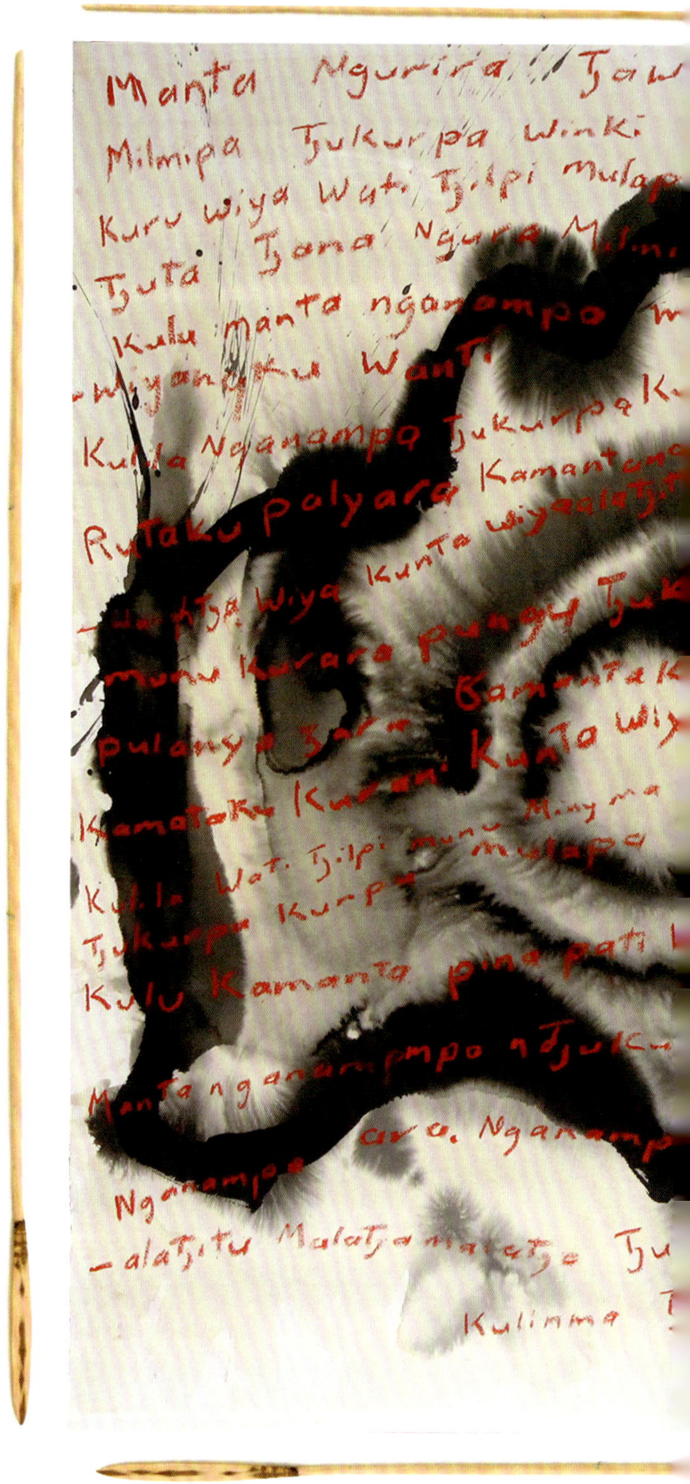

Kurantja Ngura
Kunpu Nyangatja
Mumu Mike Williams

Walkatjunanyi
Writing as artform

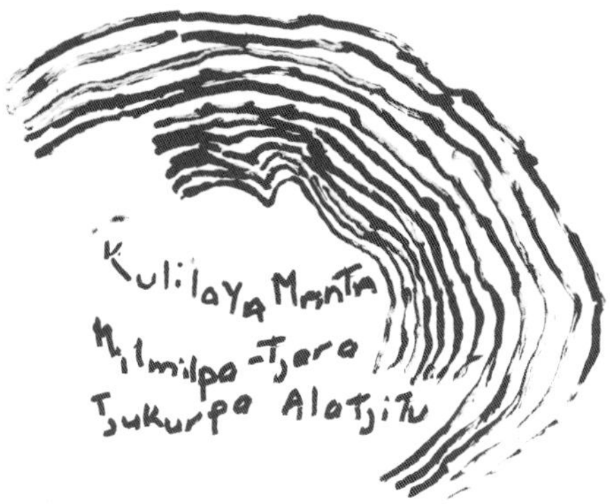

Ngayulu nganmanyitja walkatjunanyi nyaa panya, paintinga like ngayuku tjukurpa, ngura ngayuku. Munu ngayulu kuwari nguwanpa kulinu. Munu nyara palunya walkatjunu panya kulintjaku. Kulintjaku, walypala, piranpa tjutangku nganmanypa ungkunyangka wirkara tjarpara kulintjaku, ai, wiru ngangatja, tjukurpa wiru. Ka nyara palula nguru ngayulu kuliningi tjukurpa nyara palunya walkatjunanyi.

When I started painting, I depicted my Tjukurpa and my home country. More recently I decided to start writing on the paintings. I began writing so that I could literally tell the story of the painting. I wanted to tell the story of how white people first came here, but in a good way. I thought of many stories to tell and I have since been writing them all down.

Mununa panya nyaapa tjukula-tjara walkatjunanyi palunya tjananya. Tjukula munu kutjupa tjinguru walkatjunkukuna, like ulpuru, kupi-kupi pitjanyi. Pitjala rockhole kurani, tjukuritja tjuta katantananyi, punu. Kurani alatjitu kupi-kupingku.

I wrote about all our different waterholes and rockholes. I wrote about rockholes and natural phenomena such as dust storms, raised by local whirlwinds. Whirlwinds and dust storms blow the sand back into waterholes and fill them up, and break branches off trees. Whirlwinds make a mess of waterholes.

Ka kutjupa tjutangku nganampa tjukurpaku ngura kutjupa nguru pitjanyi, like painytja panya, Captain Cook. Paluru tjana pitjangi pautangka munu paluru tjana, paluru tjana like kupi-kupi purunypa, kupi-kupi purunypa pitjala kuranu.

Our Tjukurpa has suffered but withstood many onslaughts; for instance, the arrival of Captain Cook. The effect of those people arriving on their boats was similar to a huge whirlwind, a whirlwind that stormed our country and caused untold damage.

Kuranu manta nganampa. Kutjupaku manta Australianya, nyiri kutjupa wangkangu munu ngunti wangkangu, munu watjanu Australianya empty. Palu wiya, tjutatjara, rockhole, tjukurpa, ngura tjuta!

Our land has been damaged now. It has also been wrongly stated by someone else, on a document, that Australia was an empty land [*terra nullius*]. But this is not true, because we have a land filled with named rockholes and an ancient cultural heritage everywhere!

Ka wiru ngaranyi. Ka nyanga palula nguru ngayulu kulinu, 'Munta uwa, wanyu ka ngayulu tjukurpa walkatjunu kulintjaku painting nguru!' Ka tjanala painting nguru nyakula nyakula tjana kulinu, ai wirunya! Piranpa nganampa tjutangku kulinu, wiya wirunya. Tjukurpa nyangatja pulka, kunpu.'

Our land is beautiful. When I heard about that I said to myself, 'Oh I see, well, hang on then, I'm going to do a painting about that!' When everyone saw my painting, they gave it good reviews and must have thought, 'Hey, that's fascinating! We white people have a lot to think about here, which is good. This is an important story.'

Page 72: Mumu Mike in 2018 working on *Kamantaku Tjukurpa wiya (The government doesn't have Tjukurpa)* commissioned by the Museum of Contemporary Art Australia for The National 2019: New Australian Art. At 300 x 600 cm, this is the biggest painting Mumu Mike made.

Walkatjunkula paintamilalpai

I just write it all down and paint it

Katangka kulini, munu walkatjunanyi. Like katangka kulira like pitja [picture], pitja puriny mananyi. Tjilpi tjuta, pampa tjuta munu ngura, munu tjitji munu walkatjunanyi. Uwa pala puriny. Like tjinguru panya tjana tourist tjuta ananyi Uluruku, munu paluru tjana katangka kulira photographamilani, malaku ankula Amirikalakutu malaku ankula kulintjikitjangku. Ka same way ngayulu katangka kulinu munu pala puriny pitja nyangu.

I ponder an issue and I write it down. In my head, I develop a visual idea, like a picture, so I turn it into a painting. I think about the senior men, the senior women, our country, our children, and I just write it all down and paint it. That's how I do it. It is just the same way that a tourist comes to Uluru and what they see becomes like a photograph in the mind, and when they go back home to America they can still see the images. In the same way, we keep our cultural heritage strongly and clearly in our minds.

Like Itjinpirila mantjintja. Munu wangkantja, munu tjilpi tjuta strong nyinanytja, munu walkatjunu.

When we got our land back at Itjinpiri, that memory stays firmly imprinted in my memory. What was said, what the strong old men did, how they behaved, that's what I paint about.

Mumu Mike Williams started working into archival maps with acrylic markers and inks in 2016. Here he is working on *Mantaku Walytja Mulapa – The True Land-owners* in the studio at Mimili Maku Arts.

Kampatjangka walkatjunkupai
Writing on canvas

Mungangka ngayulu tea tjikira kulilpai tjukurpa. Tjukurpa katangka palu mungawinki ali pakara mai ngalkura tjukurpa panya palunya ngayulu walkatjunkupai. Nyiri nguru walkatjunkula wiyaringkula tjukurpa panya paluru tjukarurulpai alanku nyankunytjaku, 'Ai, tjukurpa nyangatja mulapa.'

Last night I was drinking tea and thinking about Tjukurpa. I thought about it all night and the next morning I got up early and had breakfast, and then I went and wrote all those thoughts down. After I had written my thoughts down on paper, I read over it to make sure it was all down straight. I was happy, 'Yes, that's the right story.'

Ngayulu kuliningi, 'Ai, munta uwa, ngayulu kuwari kampatjangka tjunanyi, tjukurpa nyangatja. Munu ngayulu walkatjunu, tjaataringu, tjukutjuku, pulkaringu, tjukurpa pulkaringu. Like-pa nyaapa, kutjupa tjutangku mai paulpai, munu putimin [put him in] nyaa tjutilpai, pulka pulkaringatjaku. Ka pulkaringkupai, ka tjunkupai apanangka [in oven], ka Anangu tjutangku ngalkupai, pala purunypa.

Then I started thinking, 'Hm, oh right, I think this story would work well painted on canvas.' So I made a start, first small, and then it got bigger and bigger, until it ended up being a huge work. It was a bit like when someone is baking bread, they put in the yeast and the dough rises and doubles in size. Well it was just like that, so when I put it in the oven and baked it, I knew that my people would be able to eat of it, to partake of it, so to speak.

Tjukurpa kuḻunypa-nguṟu nganana walkatjunanyi Aṉangungku nyakula kulintjaku, munta uwa.

So from small ideas I can paint a large work, which will be highly visible for my people to read and understand the message.

Ngurkatanama
Tjukurpa Munu Manta
Anangu Maru Tjutaku
nyangatjo

Aalpiri nyuwana

A new aalpiri

Aalpiri nyuwana purunypa. Iriti tjana aalpiringku pailpai: kutju anku wiya; maluku kutju ankunytja wiya, tjungu, tjungu anama, munuya malaku pitjaku ngura kutu. aalpiri wangkapai. Tjananya atunymanykupai. Ka kuwari nguwanpa ngaltutjara, aalpiri wiya. Palu ngananna aalpiri purunypa kuwari wangkanyi nyiringka. Tjukurpa tjunkula kulintjaku. Ngaltutjara.

There is a new way of transmitting news. Historically we have always transmitted instructions by a speech style known to us as aalpiri: for instance, do not go to such and such by yourself; do not go hunting alone; always go together; always come home again safely with the people you went with. Those instructions were passed on through aalpiri. It is a community safety mechanism. Nowadays, sadly, we are mostly deprived of aalpiri, as it hardly ever happens. Our new way of transmitting instructional news is via writing. We write down what we need to be known. Poor things.

Tjiti-kutu [City] wangkanyi: Nyangatja nyura kulini? Anangu tjutaku manta. Panya ngayulu nganala, Melbourne-ta, kulintja pitjangu [Non-Indigenous students who travel to APY with the mentoring project] munu-ya painting ngayuku nyangangi. Ka ngayulu wangkangi panya nyaapa, nyura kulu uti pitjama kimuniti-kutu [Community] munu nintiringama nganampa ara, nganampa kaltja. Munu tjungungku pakanma, uwa. Ka tjana rawa pitjapai, Antara-lakutu, kutjupa pitjapai Fregonku, munu tjungu kulilpai. Ai wirunya.

To you all in the city: Are you getting my message? This is Aboriginal land. Recently I was with some non-Indigenous students who travelled from Melbourne to the APY Lands with a mentoring project, and they were looking at one of my paintings. I was talking to them, and I said, 'You ought to visit all our communities and learn more about our ways of life and our culture. We must walk together. Oh yes.'

Ka kuwari aaḻpiri puṟunypa ngayulu wangkanyi, painting-ngka, tjukurpa. Kuulitja tjuṯangku, tjitji tjuṯangku kulintjaku. Munu tjinguṟu Canberra-lakutu tjunanyi tjukurpa, ka kulini, 'Munta uwa, nganaṉa watarku nyinangi, munu tjana tjaataṟira-lta walkatjunanyi kulini. Uwa.

So I consider my paintings to be like a kind of informative aaḻpiri speech style, but in a painting filled with stories. I want all schoolchildren to read them. They ought to be put in Canberra, where I hope the readers think to themselves, 'Oh goodness me, I've been unaware of all this until now. I'm just starting to understand, now I'm reading these texts.' Yes, indeed.

Anangu Tjuta Manta Waltja Mulapa
Munu Tjana Anganyanganyi Tjanampa
Tjukurpa Mantangka ngaranytja Tjuta
Kamantaku Tjukurpa Wiya Maningiku
Tjukurpa Wiya Kutjupangku nginti Waltjaringany
Mantaku Anangu Tjutaku Mantaka Ngarda
Kunta Wiya alatjitu Kamanta nginti Waltjaringku
Wiyanku Wanti Ananguku nguraka Maningiku
Tjukurpa Wiya anguku Tjukurpangka
Katu Tjukuritjangka Manta Milmilpa
Kulinma Tjukurpa Nyangatja
Kunpa Alatjitu
AUSTRALIA
LAND TENURE
EDITION 1 1993
Mumu Mike Williams
AUSLIG

Anangu tjuta manta walytja mulapa munu tjana anga nyanganyi tjanampa Tjukurpa mantangka ngaranytja tjuta. Kamantaku Tjukurpa wiya. Maningiku Tjukurpa wiya. Kutjupangku ngunti walytjaringanyi mantaku Anangu tjutaku mantaku ngarala kunta wiya alatjitu. Kamanta ngunti walytjangku wiyangku wanti. Ananguku nguraku maningiku Tjukurpa wiya. Ananguku Tjukurpangka katu Tjukuritjangka manta miilmiilpa. Kulinma Tjukurpa nyangatja kunpu alatjitu.

Aboriginal people are the true owners of this land. They look after the land and their Law and culture. The government is not part of our Law and culture. Mining companies are not part of our Law and culture. If someone else claims ownership of Aboriginal land, it's a lie, and they've got no shame. The government can't say they own this land, that's not true. Mining on Aboriginal land isn't part of our Law and culture. Mining destroys our sacred sites. Listen to this strong story.

Mapa Wiya, 2017
Mumu Mike Williams
acrylic marker pen on found map
89 x 98 cm
Sims Dickson Collection

Before Captain Cook, before whitefellas came, Aboriginal people always knew their country, and their sacred sites. That's why we're painting over the names of places, and the borders and boundaries on the maps – they're not ours, we know our own land. I've written in Pitjantjatjara:

Kulilaya manta miiḻmiiḻpa tjara Tjukurpa alatjiṯu. Ka wati tjilpi tjuṯangku angakanyini manta munu Tjukurpa kuṉpu.

Listen everybody, this land is very sacred and has been since the time of Creation. We senior men are strongly protecting our land, our Law and our cultural heritage.

Tjukurpa Kuṉpu (Strong Law and Culture), 2017
Mumu Mike Williams and Willy Muntjantji Martin
ink and synthetic polymer paint on found maps (backed on dibond and acrylic)
175 x 188 cm
Fondation Opale

Pages 86–7: Mumu Mike Williams working on *Kamantaku Tjukurpa wiya (The government doesn't have Tjukurpa)* for the Museum of Contemporary Art Australia, 2018.

KULiLAYA MANTA Milmipa
Tjara. Tjukurpa ALATjiTU KA
MANTA
WATi Tjilpi Tjutangku Angakanyini
MUNU TJUKURPA KUNPU
Willy Martin
Mumu Mike Williams

Aaḻpiri nyuwana

Working on mailbags

Lita iyalpai
Writing letters

Nganana walkatjunkupai. Walypala titja watjalpai, 'Nyuntumpa lita (letter) iyala.' Ka nganana lita iyalpai Fregontakutu, munu Amataku tjanampa lita iyalpai. Munu tjaatara nintiringangi. Ka tjukurpa nganampa kuwari lita purunypa, you know, walkatjunanyi kulintjaku. Tjana piruku tjaatarinytjaku.

We used to write all the time, and our whitefella teachers suggested to us, 'Why not write some letters.' So we used to send letters to Fregon and Amata. That's how we learnt to write letters. Our Tjukurpa today is documented in the form of books and essays, just like letters, you know, it is written down and can be read. We have started a new tradition of literacy.

Tjinguru ngayulu tjukurpa nyara palula ara tawaritja tjara walkatjunanyi munu ngayulu pipangka tjunanyi, ka pipangka palya wiyaringkula ngayulu tjinguru ilpulungka munu iyani, ngayuku malpakutu, ka paluru alara nyakula, 'Ai! Munta uwa!' Kulini, 'Uwa ngayuku tjamu kawankatingu. Uti ngayulu malakungku mantjinma ara nyanga palumpa.'

Let's say I write down an account of the tawaritja lifestyle on paper, and when I finish writing I put the paper into an envelope, and then send it away to my friend. He would open it and read, 'Oh! Brilliant!' He'd really like it, because he'd be worrying, 'I'm losing my grandson. I need to find him and get him back on track.'

black tea
black tea

Mailbag wirunya
Mailbags are a great medium

Ngayulu unngu nyinangi, nyangangka [Mimili Maku Art Centre], munu mailbag panya nyangu, 'Ai, nyangatja panya wirunya,' – panya watingku mailbagi katintja – 'Uti ngayulu tjukurpa walkatjunama mailbagingka, tjana kulintjaku munu katintjaku ngura kutjupa tjuta kutu, tjakultjunykunytjaku. Uwa.' Ka mailbagi nguru mantjilpai, munta nyangatja nyuntumpa letter ka letter ritamilala nyakula kulilpai, ai, letter ngayuku iyanu waltjangku, familyngku.

I was working in Mimili Maku Arts centre, when I spied an empty mailbag, and I thought to myself, 'Hey, this is brilliant,' – a man had brought the mailbag in – 'I should paint a message on this mailbag, a kind of reverse message for him to take back out with him, as a message to the world. Yes.' I envisaged the mailbag being posted along on a journey, just exactly like a letter that has been written and then read. And yes, so I sent it out into the world with a message on it from me and my family.

Ka ngayulu kuliningi nyara palula, ai, ngayulu tjinguru mailbagingka warkariwa, walkatjunkuku letter purunypa iyani ngura tjuta kutu. Ka katinyi watingku katinyi mailbag, katinyi kuulakutu, kapmanta kutu, munu tjinguru Mirikala [America] tjanala kutu, tjana kulu kulintjaku, ai, ngaltutjara, tjinguru nganampa ngura kulu kura-kurani.

Pages 94–5: Mumu Mike Williams working on *Kamantaku Tjukurpa wiya (The government doesn't have Tjukurpa)* for the Museum of Contemporary Art Australia, 2018.

I decided that I would work on more mailbag paintings, and send them away like letters, far and wide. That man has continued to post my mailbags out into the world, to schools, to the government, and maybe even to America. People all around the world can now read my messages and learn about my culture and maybe even come to understand what they might be losing from their culture too.

Ka mailbagi nyangatja wiṟu nyangatja. Uwa, kutjupangku nyanganyi [mailbag] munu, ngayulu nyangatja payamilani, munu katinyi. Overseas. Munu gallery palumpangka tjunanyi, ka kutjupangku pitjanyi munu, ai, ritamilala nyanganyi.

Mailbags are a great medium. I hope that people will see my mailbags and decide to buy them and take them overseas, to hang them in their galleries, so more and more people can read and learn from my messages on them.

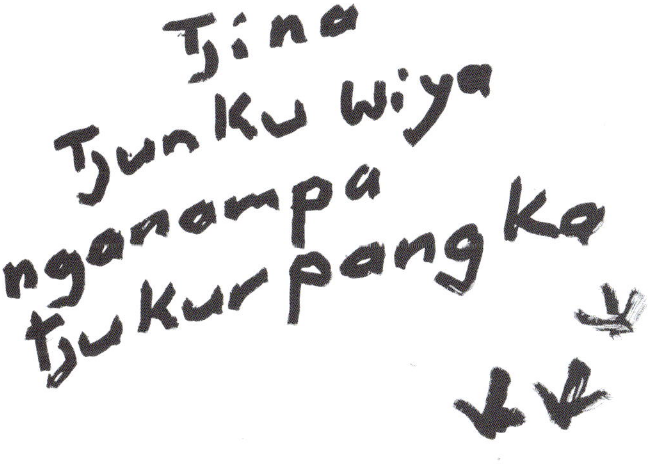

HEFT OR MISUSE OF THIS BAG
IS A CRIMINAL OFFENCE
PENALTIES APPLY

Left-hand panel:

Anangu maru tjutaku, Australia-nya manta munu Tjukurpa.

Theft or misuse of this manta munu Tjukurpa is a criminal offence. Penalties apply.

Nyaa manta?

Wiya, Tjukurpa pulka tjuta ngaranyi mantangka panya, wati tjilpi munu pampa ninti pulka Tjukurpaku.

Aboriginal people, Australian land, Law and culture

Theft or misuse of this land and culture is a criminal offence. Penalties apply.

What is land rights?

This is the old men and women's land. They're wise. They know their culture and heritage.

Right-hand panel:

Manta nyanga nganampaku, Australia-nya Tjukurpa kulu ngaranyi

Manta munu Tjukurpa

Theft or misuse of this manta munu Tjukurpa is a criminal offence.

Penalties apply.

Tjilpi munu pampa tjana ninti pulka mulapa mantaku munu Tjukurpaku.

Ka kutjupangku tjinguru Tjukurpa kutitjunanyi manta Tjukurpa winki.

Paluru tjilpi munu pampa wiyanmananyi munu ananyi tjukuritja winki kutu.

Our land, Australian culture and heritage

Land, Law and culture

Theft or misuse of this land and culture is a criminal offence.

Penalties apply.

The old men and women are very knowledgeable about the land and culture.

Outside forces often risk damaging the sacred places, but the senior people refuse to relinquish their custodianship over their sacred sites.

Australia-ku Tjurkpa, 2016
Mumu Mike Williams, Sammy Dodd (spear)
ink and acrylic on canvas mailbags with kulata (spear) made from kulata (spearbush) and mulga, malu pulyka (kangaroo tendon) and kiti (mulga leaf resin)
116 x 189 cm (diptych)
Private collection
Photo: Araluen Arts Centre

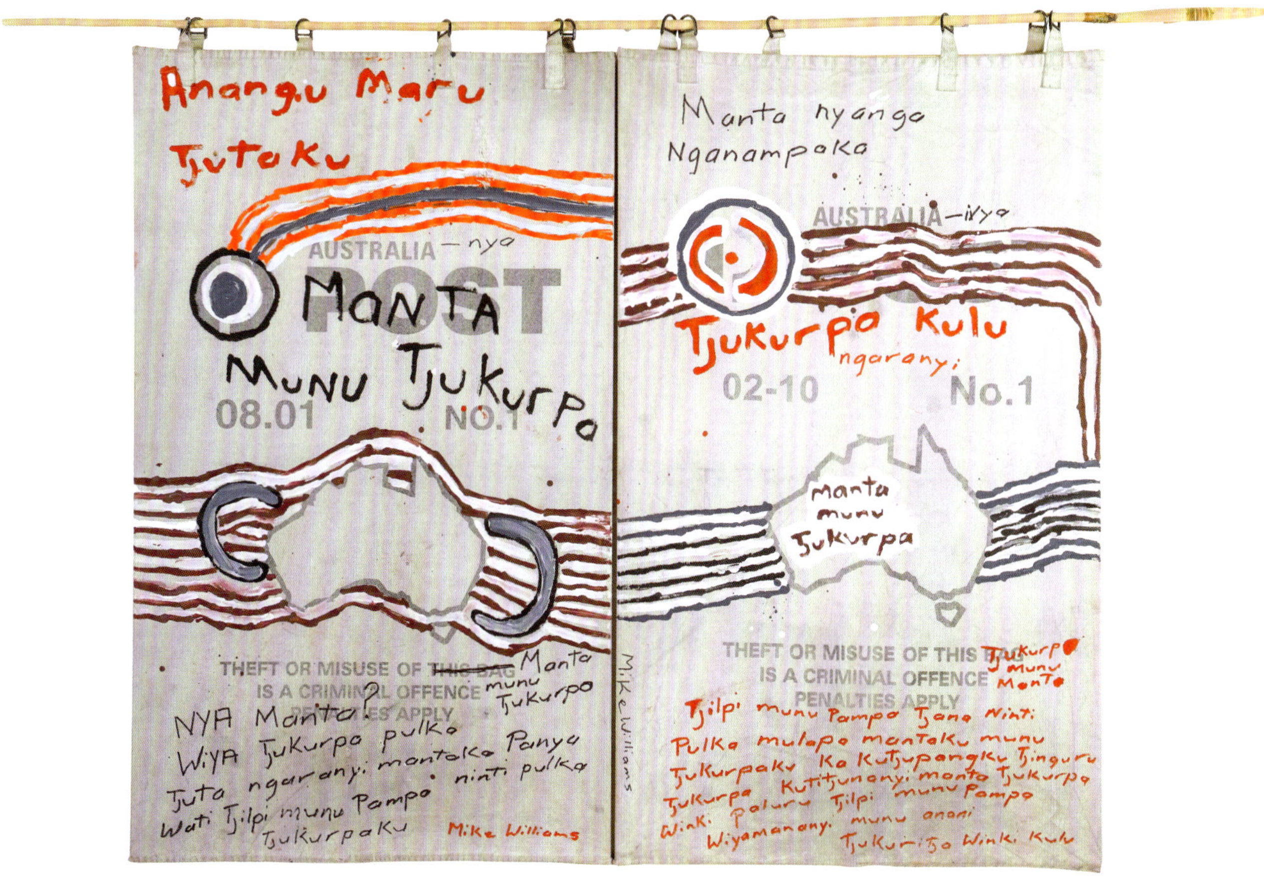

Anangu Maru Tjutaku
AUSTRALIA—nya
POST
MANTA
Munu Tjukurpa
08.01
NO.1
THEFT OR MISUSE OF THIS BAG
IS A CRIMINAL OFFENCE
PENALTIES APPLY
Manta munu Tjukurpa
NYA Manta?
Mike Williams
Manta nyanga Nganampaka
AUSTRALIA—nya
Tjukurpa Kulu ngaranyi
02-10
No.1
Manta munu Tjukurpa
THEFT OR MISUSE OF THIS
IS A CRIMINAL OFFENCE
PENALTIES APPLY
Tjukurpa munu Manta

TJUKURPA TITUTJARA
MALATJAMALATJA
AUSTRALIA
PALYA?
NGARANYI
TJUTAKU
THEFT OR MISUSE OF THIS BAG MANTA
IS A CRIMINAL OFFENCE
PENALTIES APPLY
MANTA NYANGATJA
TJUKURPA TJUTA-TJARA
NGARANYI
Mumu Mike Williams

Tjukurpa tiṯutjara ngaṟanyi maḻatja maḻatja tjuṯaku.
Australia, palya?
Theft or misuse of this manta is a criminal offence.
Penalties apply.
Manta nyangatja Tjukurpa tjuṯa tjara ngaṟanyi.

Our cultural heritage stands strong for future generations.
Australia, do you understand?
Theft or misuse of this land is a criminal offence.
Penalties apply.
This land will always be rich in Tjukurpa.

Postbag Painting, 2017
Mumu Mike Williams, Sammy Dodd (spear)
synthetic polymer paint and ink on canvas mailbags with kuḻaṯa (spear) made from spearbush, mulga, maḻu pulyku (kangaroo tendon) and kiṯi (mulga leaf resin)
198 x 122 cm
Fondation Opale
Photo: Fondation Opale/Vincent Girier DuFournier

Manta nyangangka ngaṟanyi Tjukurpa kuṉpu tjilpi tjuṯaku, palya?
Australia pina aḻariwa munu Kulinma.
Theft or misuse of this manta munu tjukurpa is a criminal offence. Penalties apply.

This land is rich in cultural heritage which the old men are protecting, understand?
Australia, open your ears and listen.
Theft or misuse of this land and its cultural heritage is a criminal offence. Penalties apply.

Postbag Painting, 2017
Mumu Mike Williams, Sammy Dodd (spear)
synthetic polymer paint and ink on canvas mailbags with kuḻaṯa (spear) made from spearbush, mulga, maḻu pulyku (kangaroo tendon) and kiṯi (mulga leaf resin), 198 x 122 cm
Fondation Opale
Photo: Fondation Opale/Vincent Girier DuFournier

MANTA
NYANGANGKA
ngaranyi
Kunpu
Tjukurpa
Tjilpi
TjutaKu
Palya?
AUSTRALIA
iNA AlariwA
Munu KuliamA
OR MISUSE OF THIS BAG
IS A CRIMINAL OFFENCE
PENALTIES APPLY
Manta
munu
Tjukurpa

ANANGUKU
TJUKURPA
KULATANGKU NINTINI
KUNPU MULAPA NGARANYI
NGURU
WATI TJILPI TJUTAGKU TJUKURPA
WALTJAGKU ATUMANANYI
WATI TJILPI
KULAKU TJUKURPA
AUSTRALIA POST
10.88
Tjukurpa Kunpu
Tjukurpa
Mumu Mike Williams

WATI Tjilpi Tjutaku Tjukurpa
Kunpu Alatjitu

[Side A]

Ananguku tjukurpa.
Kulatangku nintini wati tjilpi
kunpu mulapa ngaranyi kulataku tjukurpa
nguru.
Wati tjilpi tjutaku tjukurpa
walytjangku atunymananyi
kulata tjilira winki tjarangku.

Anangu Law.
The old men are teaching with spears. The old Laws about spears are very strong and come from the times of the Tjukurpa.
All the senior men are holding strongly onto their own Tjukurpa and Law around bundles of spears.

Tjukurpa kunpu.

Our Law and culture stands strong.

[Side B]

Wati tjilpi tjutaku Tjukurpa kunpu alatjitu.

The old men's Law and culture is very powerful.

Ngura (Country), 2017
Mumu Mike Williams, Willy Muntjantji Martin, Sammy Dodd (spears)
acrylic, ink and acrylic marker pen on canvas mailbags with kulata (spear) made from punu (wood), malu pulyku (kangaroo tendon) and kiti (mulga leaf resin)
116 x 142 x 2 cm
Art Gallery of New South Wales
Purchased with funds provided by the Aboriginal Collection Benefactors' Group 2017
Photos: Jackson Lee

[Side A]

Wati tjilpi tjutaku Tjukurpa kunpu alatjitu.

The old men's Law is strong and powerful.

[Side B]

Ananguku manta nganampa lipiwanu Tjukurpa winki tjara.
Kulilya manta miilmiilpa tjara Tjukurpa alatjitu.

The whole of this wide land belongs to Aboriginal people and all of it holds Tjukurpa and cultural heritage.
Theft or misuse of this Tjukurpa is a criminal offence. Penalties apply.
You must understand that the land is sacred with Tjukurpa.

Ngura (Country), 2017
Mumu Mike Williams, Willy Muntjantji Martin, Sammy Dodd (spears)
acrylic, ink and acrylic marker pen on canvas mailbags, with kulata (spear) made from spearbush, mulga, malu pulyku (kangaroo tendon) and kiti (mulga leaf resin)
142 x 116 cm
Private collection
Photos: Jackson Lee

AUSTRALIA
Pina Alangku
Kulila Wati Tjilpi
Tjuta Mayayatja
THEFT OR MISUSE OF THIS BAG
IS A CRIMINAL OFFENCE
PENALTIES APPLY
Mumu Mike Williams

Pina aḻangku kulila. Wati tjilpi tjuṯa mayatjaya.
Theft or misuse of this manta munu Tjukurpa is a criminal offence.
Penalties apply.

Open your ears and listen. The senior old men are the ultimate bosses.
Theft or misuse of this land and its cultural heritage is a criminal offence.
Penalties apply.

Pina Aḻangku, 2018
Mumu Mike Williams, Sammy Dodd (spears)
synthetic polymer paint and ink on canvas mailbags with kuḻaṯa (spear) made from spearbush, mulga, maḻu pulyku (kangaroo tendon) and kiṯi (mulga leaf resin)
180 x 122 cm
Private collection

Australia-ku Tjukurpaku wati tjilpi munu minyma tjana ninti munu Tjukurpa kanyilpai tjitji maḻatja maḻatja tjuṯa nintintjaku Tjukurpa tiṯutjara.
Australia, pina aḻangku kulinma.
Pampul wiya.
Theft or misuse of this Tjukurpa is a criminal offence. Penalties apply.
Theft or misuse of this land is a criminal offence. Penalties apply.
Nganampa wangka, nganampa aṟa, nganampa Tjukurpa kuṉpu tiṯutjara alatjiṯu.
Kulila munuya nintiriwa, palya?

Australia's Tjukurpa is held and managed by our senior men and women.
They are the ones who are keeping our Tjukurpa strong for new generations of children coming up, and will continue to teach it, always.
Australia, open your ears and remember this.
Do not damage our cultural heritage.
Theft or misuse of this Tjukurpa is a criminal offence. Penalties apply.
Theft or misuse of this land is a criminal offence. Penalties apply.
Our language, our cultural identity and our Tjukurpa are strong and enduring.
Listen and learn, okay?

Postbag Painting, 2017
Mumu Mike Williams, Sammy Dodd (spears)
synthetic polymer paint on canvas mailbag; wood, kangaroo tendon
218 x 378 cm (overall)
Artbank collection, purchased 2017

KU Tjukurpaku Wati Tjilpi munu Minyma Tjana Ninti
munu Jukurpa Kanyilpai Tjitji
Mnlatja Malatja Tjuta
Nintintjikitjangku Tjukurpa
Titutjara
Australia
Pina Alangku kulinma
PAMPUL WIYA
No. 1
NGANAMPA WANGKA
Nganampa Ara
Ngampa Tjukurpa Kunpu
Titutjara Ala Tjitu-
Kulila
MUNUYA
NINTIRIWA
PALYA?
Mumu Mike Williams

KUlilAYA
MANTA
MILPATJARA
AUSTRALIA
08.03
NO.
Tjukurpa
THEFT OR MISUSE OF THIS BAG
IS A CRIMINAL OFFENCE
PENALTIES APPLY
TJUKURPA
Australia
Alangku
Kulinma
ALATJITU
AUSTRALIA
Kutitjunku Wiyangku
Wantima Manta
ngananpa
08:04
NO. WIYA
THEFT OR MISUSE OF THIS
Manta
IS A CRIMINAL OFFENCE
PENALTIES APPLY
KUNPU

Kulilaya manta miil̲miil̲pa tjara Tjukurpa alatjit̲u kun̲pu.
Australia pina al̲angku kulinma.
Kulinin kutitjunku wiyangku wantima manta nganampa.

Listen up! Our land is sacred and our Law and Culture is strong.
Theft or misuse of this Tjukurpa (Law and Culture) is a criminal offence.
Australia. Open your ears and listen!
Do you hear. Never, ever steal our land.
Theft or misuse of this land is a criminal offence.

Postbag Painting, 2016
Mumu Mike Williams, Sammy Dodd (spear)
acrylic, ink and acrylic marker pen on canvas mailbags, with kul̲at̲a (spear) made from spearbush, mulga, mal̲u pulyku (kangaroo tendon) and kit̲i (mulga leaf resin)
3 panels each 116 x 70 cm, kul̲at̲a 250 cm long
Sims Dickson Collection

Ngunti walytjaringku kurantja wantima. Tjukurpa wiyangku. Pampuntja wiya.

Do not pretend to own what is not yours. Never destroy Tjukurpa Law. Do not touch.

Iyukuta Tjukurpa, 2018
Mumu Mike Williams
acrylic on linen and canvas mailbag
196.5 x 196.5 cm
Art Gallery of New South Wales
Photo: Mim Stirling, Art Gallery of New South Wales
Finalist in the Wynne Prize 2018, Art Gallery of New South Wales

Ngunti
WALtjarikula Tjukurpa
Kurantja
WANTima
Wiyangku
pampuntja
Wiya
MISUSE OF THIS BAG
Mumu Mike Williams

Post
Ngannapa

AUSTRALIA
IS A CRIMINAL OFFENCE
MANTA

Ruta Pulyantja
Manta

Nganampa Tjukurpa kun̲pu ngar̲anyi tjitji mal̲atja tjut̲aku.

Our Law and Culture is still strong, for all the children who come after.

Pages 114–15: *Ngura (Country),* 2017
Mumu Mike Williams, Willy Muntjantji Martin and Sammy Dodd (spears)
acrylic, ink and acrylic marker pen on canvas mailbags, with kul̲at̲a (spears)
116.5 x 338 cm (diptych)
Araluen Art Collection, acquired from *Desert Mob 2017*
Photo: Araluen Arts Centre

Pages 116–17: Mumu Mike Williams working on *Kamantaku Tjukurpa wiya (The government doesn't have Tjukurpa)* for the Museum of Contemporary Art Australia, 2018.

Overleaf: Mumu Mike Williams working on *Kamantaku Tjukurpa wiya (The government doesn't have Tjukurpa)* in his studio in Mimili, 2018. Photo: Mimili Maku Arts

Maru Tjukurpa
Titutjara alatjitu ngarany
Tjitji malatjamalatja
tjutaku Kulu Tjukurpa Kunpu
Alatjitu.
Kamanta Nguntí Waltjaringanyi
munu Manta Tjukurpa
Kurani Kunta Wiyangku
Alatjitu
Mumu Mike Williams

Maruku Tjukurpa titutjara alatjitu ngaranyi tjitji malatja malatja tjutaku kulu Tjukurpa kunpu alatjitu.
Kamanta ngunti walytjaringanyi munu manta Tjukurpa kurani. Kunta wiyangku alatjitu.
Manta nyanga miilmiilpa tjara wantima tjawantja wiyangku.
Anangu No 1, Tjukurpa No 1
Kulinma, munuya pitjala nyangama wati tjilpi tjutangku atunytju kanyilpai.
Ruta palyantja wiyangku manta miilmiilpa wanungku nganampa Tjukurpa kurani.
Kamantaku Tjukurpa wiya.
Nganampa manta. Nganampa Tjukurpa. Nganampa ara. Tjukurpa miilmiilpa tjara.

Black-skinned Aboriginal people have always had powerful Tjukurpa Dreaming Law and have passed it down through generations since time began.
The government simply cannot claim ownership of this land and must never destroy cultural heritage sites. The shame of it.
Do not destroy sacred sites or dig up the land around them.
The first people, the true culture
Listen, if you come here, you must accept that the Law of our land is under the control of our senior men.
Do not plan to build roads in the vicinity of sacred sites, because of the risk of destroying Tjukurpa.
The government doesn't have a Dreaming.
This is our land. Our Tjukurpa. Our cultural heritage. Our Tjukurpa is sacred.

Kamantaku Tjukurpa wiya (The government doesn't have Tjukurpa), 2018
Mumu Mike Williams, Sammy Dodd (spears)
synthetic polymer, ink and acrylic marker pen on canvas mailbags and linen, with kulata (spear) made from kulata (spearbush) and mulga, malu pulyku (kangaroo tendon) and kiti (mulga leaf resin)
300 x 600 cm
Image courtesy the artist and Museum of Contemporary Art Australia
Photo: Jessica Maurer

Ruta Palyantja Wiyangku
Manta Milmilpa Wanunku
Nganampa Tjukurpan Kurmi
Kamantaku Tjukurpa Wiya
Nganampa Manta
Nganampa Tjukurpa
Nganampa Ara
Tjukurpa Milmilpa
Tjara

AUSTRALIA
POST
No.1
THEFT OR MISUSE OF THIS BAG
IS A CRIMINAL OFFENCE
PENALTIES APPLY

Opposite: A freshly painted tjukul̲a (rockhole).
Detail from *Kamantaku Tjukurpa wiya (The government doesn't have Tjukurpa)*, 2018.

Kuḻaṯa

The old men and their spears are guarding their culture

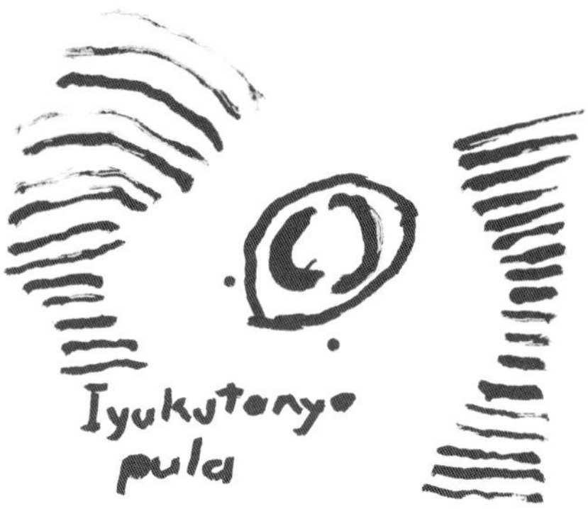

Ngayulu tjukurpa tjuka<u>r</u>urungku wangkapai.

I tell my story straight and true.

Tjukurpa iriti, ngayulu wiyangka. Ngayulu i<u>t</u>i wirkanu, ka ngayulu kulinu Tjukurpa. Ngayulu nyangu munu ngayulu pampu<u>n</u>u. Kuwari ngayulu pu<u>t</u>u changemila<u>n</u>i. Tjukurpa nganampa *Land Rights Act* kapamantaku wiya. Nganampa Tjukurpa nga<u>r</u>anyi manta nganampangka. Tjukurpa tju<u>t</u>a. Youngfella tju<u>t</u>a nintiringkunytjaku.

Tjukurpa comes from the deep past, from the time before my birth. After I was born, I was taught the Tjukurpa. I have seen places and I have touched things. I can't change our history. Our *Land Rights Act* does not belong to the government. The Act is there to protect our sacred lands. Filled with Tjukurpa Law. Filled with knowledge for young men to learn.

Palula ngu<u>r</u>u ngayulu walkatjunanyi. A<u>n</u>angu kutjupa tju<u>t</u>aku, pi<u>r</u>anpa kutjupa tju<u>t</u>aku ngurkantankunytjaku, 'Munta uwa! Tjukurpa pu<u>l</u>ka!' Wati tjilpi tju<u>t</u>aku kutju wiya palu<u>r</u>u, minyma tju<u>t</u>aku ku<u>l</u>u ku<u>l</u>u, Tjukurpa pu<u>l</u>ka.

This is what I depict in my paintings. For other A<u>n</u>angu to read and learn from and also for non-Aboriginal people to read and learn to recognise, 'Oh I understand now! This is a sacred land!' Our sacred land is not just belonging to the old men, it belongs to the women as well. They too have a powerful Tjukurpa Law.

Ka nyara palunya ngayulu pipa palunya tjunanyi walkatjunanyi nintintjaku. Ka ngayulu usemilani Tjukurpa, ngayuku tjamuku tjanampa Tjukurpa. Ngayuku weapon, Law, Tjukurpa. Irititja power pulka tjara. Tjana kulata, tjamunya tjana kulata wiyangka weak. Pala palunya Tjukurpa munu kulata kanyini tjanampa weapon pulka.

It is because of my knowledge that I now depict so many works on paper. I use the Tjukurpa, which was given to me by my grandfather. This is my weapon, my Law, my Tjukurpa. The ancient power is as potent as ever. They carried spears, the old men, and without his spears my grandfather would have been weak. But with his spears and his Law, my grandfather had tremendous weapons.

Panya ngayulu painting-ngka tjuta [Marutjuku wangka] ngananya, munu ngayulu walkatjunu like Maralinga. Ngayulu palumpa tjukurpa, palumpa tjukurpa kulinu munu ngayulu walkatjunu Maralinganya tjara. Munu ngayulu walkatjunu likepa nyaa panya kulata panya, kulata tjuta pintji purunypa, ka nganampa tjukuritja tjuta unngu ngaranyi, unngu ka pintji purunypa kulata. Anga kanyini.

I have documented in my paintings many stories that my brother-in-law [Yami Lester] told me, such as stories about Maralinga. I listened closely to what he had to say, and I wrote down a lot about what he told me about Maralinga. I have documented his ideas about a fence made of spears, surrounding and protecting our culture and country. Imagine a fence made of spears. It would be the perfect protection.

Page 120: Witjiti George, Taylor Cooper, Mumu Mike Williams and Willy Muntjantji Martin in front of the Kulata Tjuta installation for TARNANTHI: Festival of Contemporary Aboriginal and Torres Strait Islander Art at the Art Gallery of South Australia, October 2017.
Photo: Rhett Hammerton

Palu ulpuru pitjapai ngayulu wangkanyi, kupikupi pulka panya. Munu waninyi kulata panya! Palulanguru nganana paintingi ngayulu tjunu malakungku piruku kulata palunya tjuta tjunkunytjaku. Kanyintjaku like rockhole, ngura pulka tjuta, tjukurpa ka nganana kuliningi nyanga palunya, strong ngaranytjikitjangku, atunymankunytjikitjangku.

I have told you about the effects of dust storms and whirlwinds. Imagine the speed and accuracy of a spear being thrown. After that, I decided to put spears in most of my paintings, so they could keep a protective force around our rockholes, sacred sites, and Tjukurpa. We still live by the same rules today, staying strong in our identity, so we can offer the best protection we can.

Kuḻaṯangku nintini watiku tjukurpa kuṉpu ngura miiḻmiiḻpa tjara munu tjukuritja uwankara kuṉpungku angakanyintjaku kuṉpungku. Kuḻaṯangku anga ngaṟanyi manta tjukuritja uwankara panya wati tjilpi uwankara kuranyitja.

The spear is our culture. We live by the spear. It's protecting our culture, our sacred sites, our heritage, our Tjukurpa – and we're protecting them strongly. The old men with their spears are standing guard, guarding their culture.

Overleaf: *Kuḻaṯangku,* 2016 (detail)
Mumu Mike Williams, Sammy Dodd (spears – not pictured)
tea, ink, acrylic and chalk pastel on 300 gsm watercolour paper, with kuḻaṯa (spear)
frame made from kuḻaṯa (spearbush) and mulga, maḻu pulyku (kangaroo tendon)
and kiṯi (mulga leaf resin)
150 x 100 cm
Artbank collection, 2016

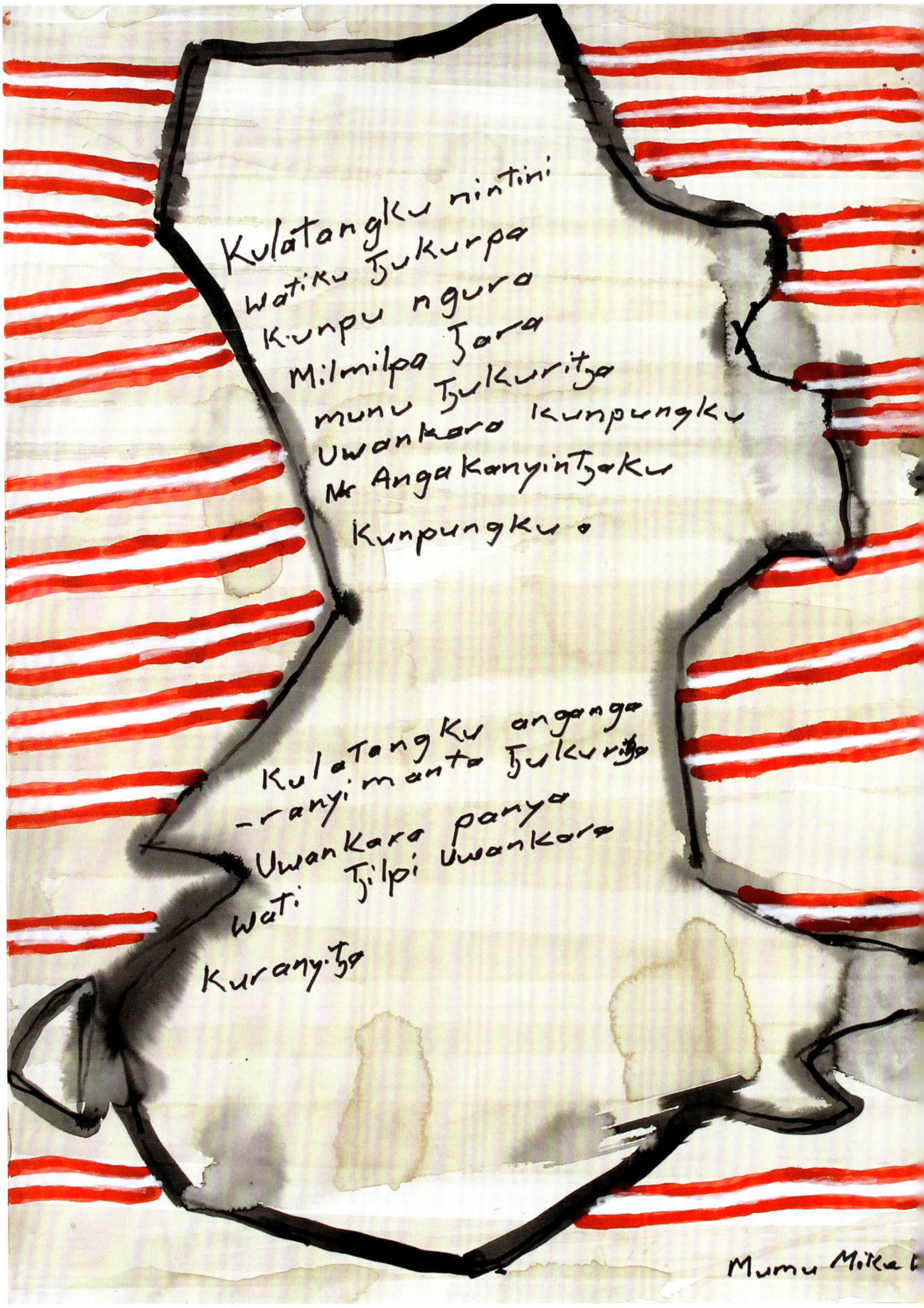
Kulatangku nintini
watiku Tjukurpa
Kunpu ngura
Milmilpa Jara
munu Tjukuritja
Uwankara kunpungku
Angakanyintjaku
Kunpungku.
Kulatangku anganga
-ranyi manta Tjukuritja
Uwankara panya
Wati Tjilpi Uwankara
Kuranyitja
Mumu Mike

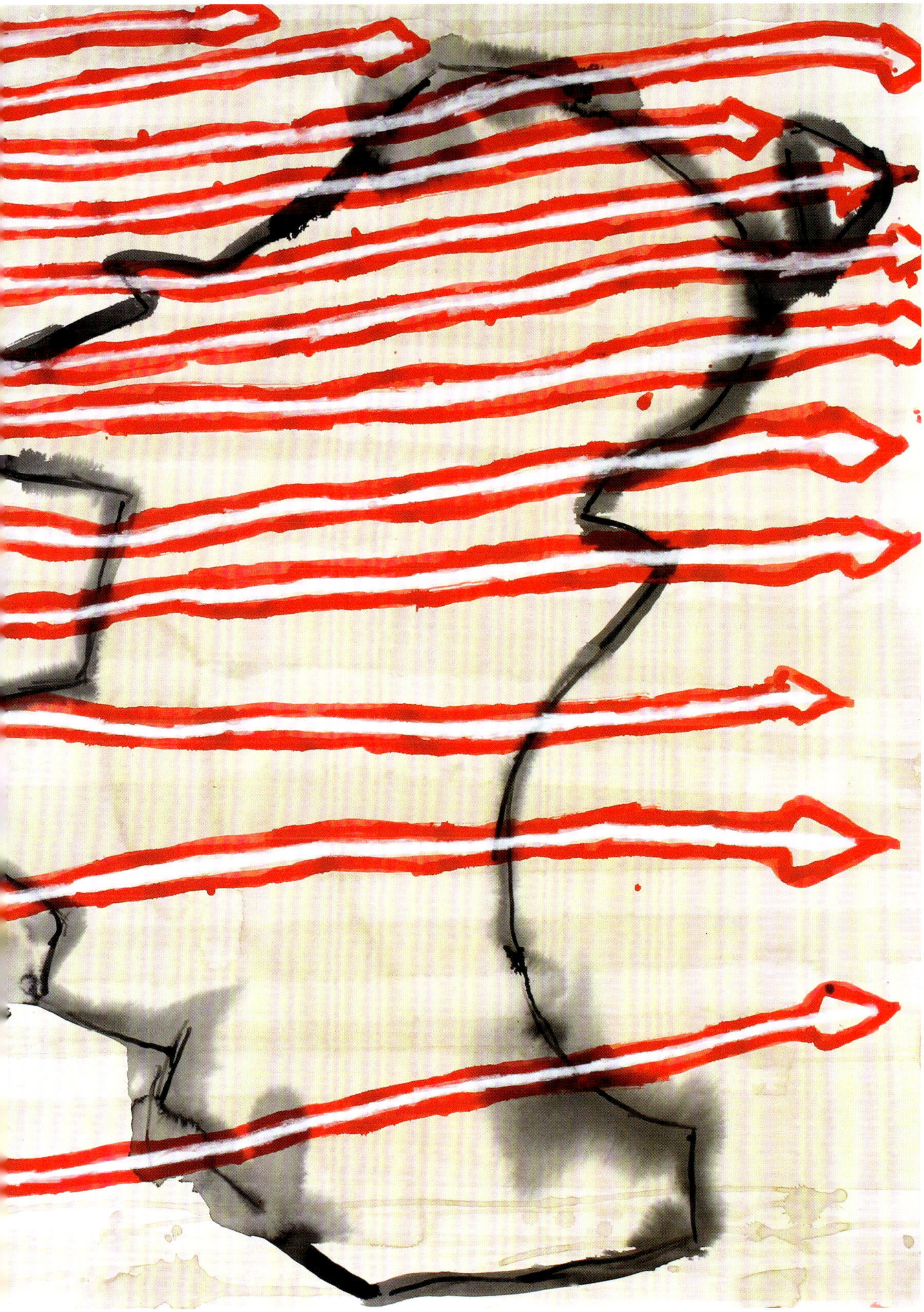

Maralinganya tjara

About Maralinga

Mimilila, ngayulu ngarangi tjitji. Munu ngayulu tuu ngayulu kulinu. Ngayulu uti kuliningi tjinguru wanampi, water snake, palu tomorrow ngayulu nyangu nyara clinic Pukatjala tjuta mulapa ngarinyi, Anangu tjuta. Ka ngayulu kuliningi nyaa? Nyaaringu nyangatja? Ka walypala missionary-ngku wheelbarrow-ngka katipai tjananya, ngaltutjara, munu tjawara paluru tjunkupai mantangka. Ka tjuta mulapa Maralingangku nyangangka kuranu.

When I was still a little child we lived in Mimili. One day I heard a noise. I heard it quite clearly but I thought it might have been a wanampi, rainbow serpent. The next day I went to Ernabella, and there at the clinic, I saw many, many Aboriginal people lying around on the ground. I was wondering, what has happened to them? What is going on? The whitefella missionary was carting the dead in a wheelbarrow and burying them in the bush. Maralinga [atomic bomb tests] killed many of our people.

Like Mimilila kunyu, pala purunypa. Ka ngayuku marutju pala purunypa tuu nyaaringu, ngaltutjara. Munu ngayuku kuntilingku paluru wangakangi, palaku nyinangi, munu nyangu, pulka, puyu puriny pitjangi, waintara anu ka palumpa mama ngunytju wiyaringu. Ka paluru nyinangi tjinguru kunkunpa ngarinyi palu wiyaringu, ngaltutjara.

Mimili was the same, the same thing happened there. My brother-in-law [Yami Lester] heard the same explosive noise, poor thing, and we all know what happened to him. My auntie, who was there, was telling me that then something enormous started coming, like a huge smoke cloud, which passed right through them all. Soon thereafter her father and mother died. They looked like they were just lying down asleep, but they had both in fact died, poor things.

Palula nguru nganana, ngayulu palatja walkatjunu kulintjaku tjana ngurkantankunytjaku, ngura munu manta. Nganampa kunpu ngaranytjaku. Pikatjararingkunytja wiya, mai nganampa pakantja kampurarpa, wiriny-wirinypa. Malu nganampa pikatjara wiya nyinantjaku, nganana kuka ngalkuntjaku. Ngayulu pulkara pukularinytjaku, kuwari nyuntula wangkara.

I have since written this story down, so that there can be no mistake about what happened, when and where on our country. So our history can be kept strong and authentic. We must stay strong and healthy, and keep eating our own wild-grown bush foods, like desert raisins and bush tomatoes. Our kangaroos have remained strong and healthy, and they are our favourite meat animals. It gives me a good feeling to be talking to you about these foods.

Ka paluru [Yami Lester] wangkapai tjukurpa pulka tjuta. Talapaunta wangkapai, radio-ngka wangkapai [HF Flying Doctor Radio], ngayuku marutjungku. Because main one. Main one, wati tjilpi tjuta. Munu minyma pampa tjuta, paluru tjana. Palu paluru tjana ninti. Ninti pulka. Mantaku, munu nguraku.

My brother-in-law [Yami Lester] used to speak out on very important matters. He'd talk over the telephone and on the HF Flying Doctor Radio [over which Mr Lester would interpret the morning's news after listening to ABC Radio morning news]. He was the main one, that old man. The old men are the most important ones. There are numerous senior women elders of great importance. They are the ones who know the Law. They are extremely knowledgeable. They know about the physical land itself, and the cultural landscape.

Kutjupara ngayulu ngayuku painting-ngka wangkapai, wangkapai ngayulu wati nguraritja, tjilpi tjutangka kulinma, ka nyanga paluru numpa one. Kulintjaku, because, panya, manta, Anangu maru-ku manta ngura pulka mulapa, tjitji tjutaku. Tjitji tjutangku pulkaringkula kulintjaku. Pulka. Ngaltutjara.

In many of my paintings I refer to the senior land-holding men, how we must heed their Law, because they are number one. We need to listen to them, because our land, our Aboriginal land is sacred, and is being held in trust for the new generations of children to come and for today's children to inherit when they are grown up. This is so important. Bless them all.

Above: Senior APY men outside Yami Lester's house; left to right: Mumu Mike Williams, Jimmy Pompey, Alec Baker, David Frank, Yami Lester, 2017.
Photo: Jackson Lee

Pages 134–5: The Kul̲at̲a Tjut̲a installation was an outcome of the ongoing Kul̲at̲a Tjut̲a (Many Spears) Project, led by senior An̲angu men, and supported by the APY Art Centre Collective. This installation for TARNANTHI included 550 suspended kul̲at̲a in the shape of a nuclear cloud as a response to the nuclear weapons testing at Emu Field and Maralinga in the far north of South Australia between 1953 and 1963.
Photo: Saul Steed

Tjukurpa nyangatja
Irati Wangkanyi
Palya?
Tjamuku munu
Kamiku ngamanypa Palya
Ngarangi Tjukurpa Winki
Palu Piranpku mantjra Juma
Irati munu iluntanu Tjuta
mulapa Nyangatja Kuranyu Emula
munu Mala Maralingkala
Nyangaka Emula 15/10/1953.
Mumu Mike Williams

Tjukurpa nyangatja iraṯi wangkanyi palya? Tjamuku munu kamiku nganmanypa palya nyangangi Tjukurpa winki. Palu piṟanpangku mantangka tjunu iraṯi munu iluntanu tjuṯa mulapa. Nyangatja kuranyu Emula munu maḻa Maralingala. Nyangangka wirkaṉu iraṯi Emula 15/10/1953.

This is an iraṯi [poison, nuclear fallout] story, okay? In the time of our ancestors everything was good on the land and they oversaw and maintained our cultural heritage well. But when whitefellas came and detonated those bombs and poisoned our land with nuclear fallout, they killed many of our people. First they poisoned Emu and later they poisoned Maralinga with their bombs. The poisoning began at Emu on 15/10/1953.

Iraṯi (Poison) Story, 2016
Mumu Mike Williams, Sammy Dodd (spears)
ink and tea on paper, spears made from kuḻaṯa (spearbush) and mulga, maḻu pulyku (kangaroo tendon) and kiṯi (mulga leaf resin)
150 x 100 cm
Collection of The University of Queensland, purchased 2016
Photo: Carl Warner

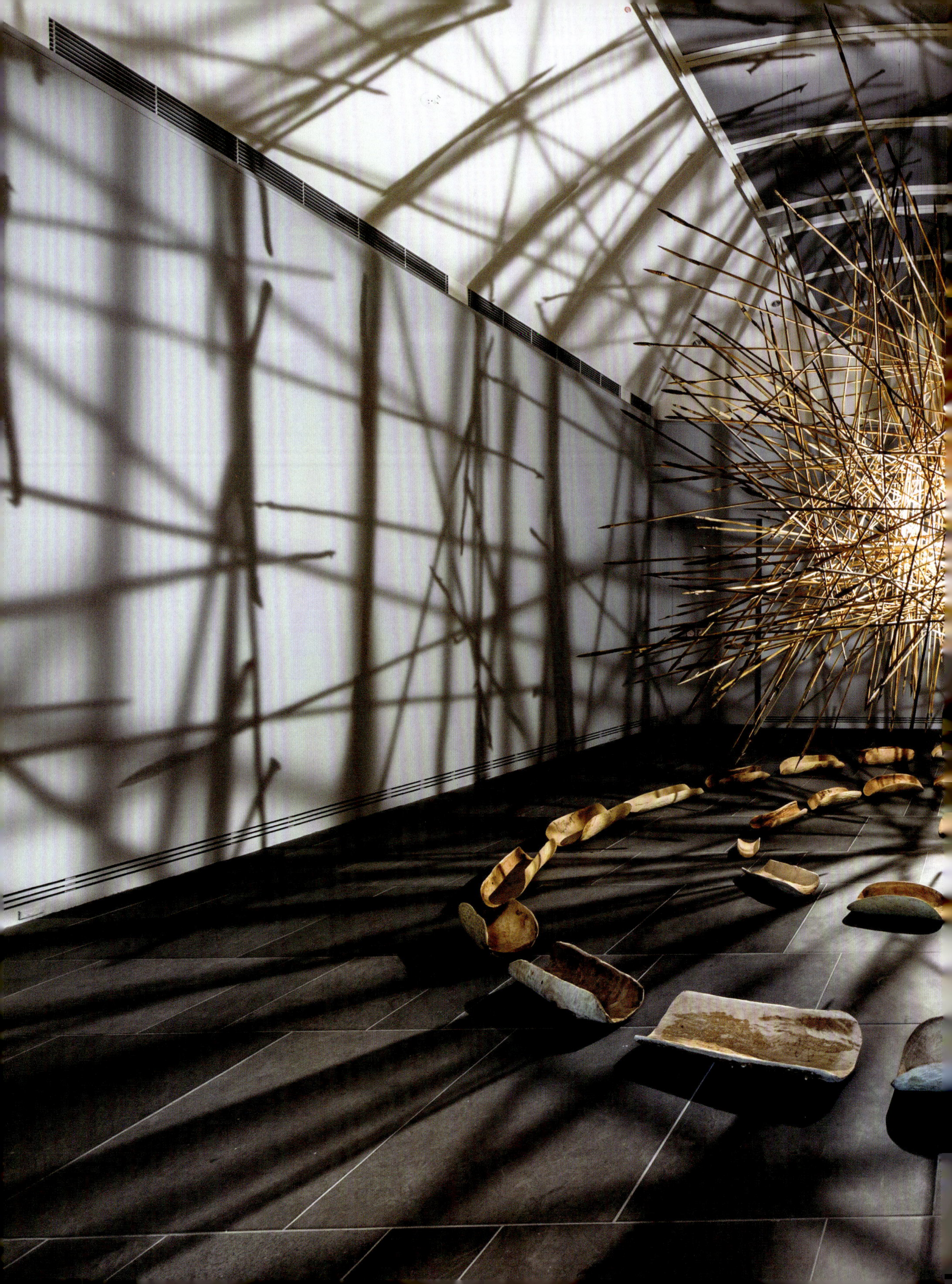

EXIT

Itjinpiri

Itjinpiri past and present

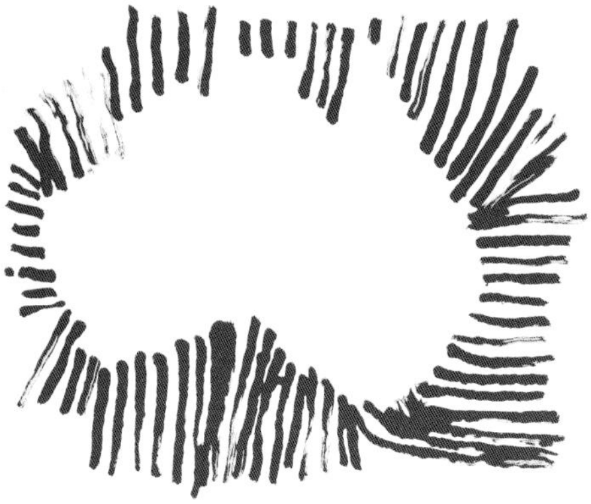

Panya iriti tjana ngura tjut̲angka mitingi wangkangi, mitingi wangkapai Amata-la tjaataringu. Munu homeland-ngka wangkapai numpa 16-ta [Wintawatanya] Amata-la parari-parari. Mimili-ku pitjapai munu tjana mitingi wangkapai, tjilpi tjut̲angku. Rawangku tjana wangkapai.

Back in the days of the fight for land rights, there were many meetings. The first was held in Amata. That's where it all started. All the homeland dwellers spoke up strongly, for instance at Wintawata No. 16, a homeland not far from Amata. The old men would travel to Mimili for meetings, and speak there.

Ka kapmantangku kulir̲a kulir̲a tjananya ungu, mal̲akungku. Munu panya nyaapa, tjilpi mulapa kunyu, ngura nganala panya, Iltur-ta tjilpi tjut̲a nyinangi unngu. Permit. Manta witinytjaku. Angakanyintjaku. Pul̲ka. Ngal̲tutjara

The government of the day, after listening to them and understanding their message, finally gave them the rights to their land a few years later. Senior old men, traditional owners from Iltur, demanded the right to the permit system, to help them hold onto their land better, and to give them the right to refuse entry if necessary. It gave them the power. Bless them.

Ngura kutju Itjinpiri. An̲angu tjut̲a Itjinpirila kutu anu, ngura kutju. Nganan̲a katingu Mr Tonkinku [Premier of South Australia] nintiringkunytjaku watiku ngurakutu munu Tjukurpa wangkangu. Palur̲u nyangu, pina kulinu. Palur̲u wangkangu, 'Ngayulu tjingur̲u put̲u wiyanmananyi. Ngayulu palya uwa wangkanyi.' Palur̲u kulinu ngura Walawurunya tjara.

Above: First Pitjantjatjara Council meeting, in Amata, 13–14 July 1976.
Ivan Baker (wearing beanie) and Mildred Yangkuyi Lyons in discussion.
Photo: Collection Pitjantjatjara Council (Penny Tweedie), Ara Irititja (AI-0036527)

Page 136: Anangu families at the dry creek bed of Itjinpiri, on 4 November 1981, the day of the offical Pitjantjatjara Land Rights handback ceremony.
Photo: Collection Jill & Allen Steel, Ara Irititja (AI-0124015) (detail)

Itjinpiri was the main place. That's why we Anangu went there, why we had the Land Rights celebration there, because it is the main place. We took Mr Tonkin [Premier of South Australia] and we showed him the special men's area, and told him the Tjukurpa. Once Mr Tonkin saw that, he knew. He said, 'I can't say might be. I have got to say yes.' He remembered. That site is a Walawuru Eagle site.

Paluru wangkangu tjinguru ngula katipai kapamantangku piruku kutitjunkunytjaku tawara nganampa manta. Nganana ninti. Nganana nyaranyi kunpu mulapa. Tjanampa wiya. Ananguku manta. Ananguku Tjukurpa. Nganana wati tjilipiku manta, ka tjitiku munu kungkaku manta. Paluru wirunya.

He told us that maybe one day a different government might try to change the Act. So we have got to be strong. So everybody knows that now, that we have got to stay strong. Hold Anangu land. Anangu Tjukurpa. It is not just the old men's land, it is the children's land and the women's land. That's the beauty of it.

Wirunya alatjitu
Speaking of a time of promise

Ngayulu nyinangi Anapalala munu ngayulu Itjinpiriku anu munu nganana karungka nyinangi. Ka nyara palula ma pitjangu ka nganana uwankara watipitjangu, munu nganana nyinangi nyara palula kutu.

I was living in Ernabella at the time when we went to Itjinpiri Creek. Everybody gathered there and we all walked across to the meeting together.

Piranpa ini nganganya, Mr Tonkin. Ngayulu painting-nkga tjunu nyanga palunya, ka kutjupangku payamilanu munu katingu, Alice Springala kutu. Ngayulu walkatjunu piranpa, Anangu maru tjuta nyinanytja. Panya ngayulu nyangakutu ngarangi, kunta-kunta yangapala. Munu ngayulu wati nyanga palunya nyangu mununa, ai, wati nyangangku ngurkantanu, Anangu maru tjutaku tjukurpa, munu paluru tjananya alatji wangkantja wiyatu nganala wangkantja wiyatu. Tjinguru, 'Ngayulu ungkuku nyuranya, paluru ngayulu promise wangkanyi, munu nyuntunya unganyi. Munu malaku nguru coming up Ayers-rockanya tjana ngaranyi.'

This man's name was Mr Tonkin. I made a painting of this event. I painted this white man and all the Anangu that were present at the time. I was there too, still a shy young man. I remember seeing this man, realising that he truly recognised Aboriginal people. They'd never been spoken to in that manner before. 'I am now returning your land to you because that was my promise to you. Here is the title. Coming up next will be the return of Ayers Rock.'

Tjukurpa Ayers-Rockanya tjana nyura manta ngalimpangka ngara ku. Ai, ai nyangatja wirunya alatjitu, Itjinpirila.

The issue of Ayers Rock was that it is to be a shared lease agreement, but still returned to the traditional owners. But oh, that was a great meeting [at Itjinpiri].

Interpreter kutjupa ngarangi Mr Thompson. Palumpa malpa. Malpa tjuta-tjara like ngayuku brother panya Albert Lennon, paluru tjana. Palumpa tjanampa malpa.

The interpreter at the Itjinpiri meeting was Punch Thompson. He worked closely [with Tonkin]. He was a good friend to all of us, and a brother to Albert Lennon and all of them. He was a friend of everybody's.

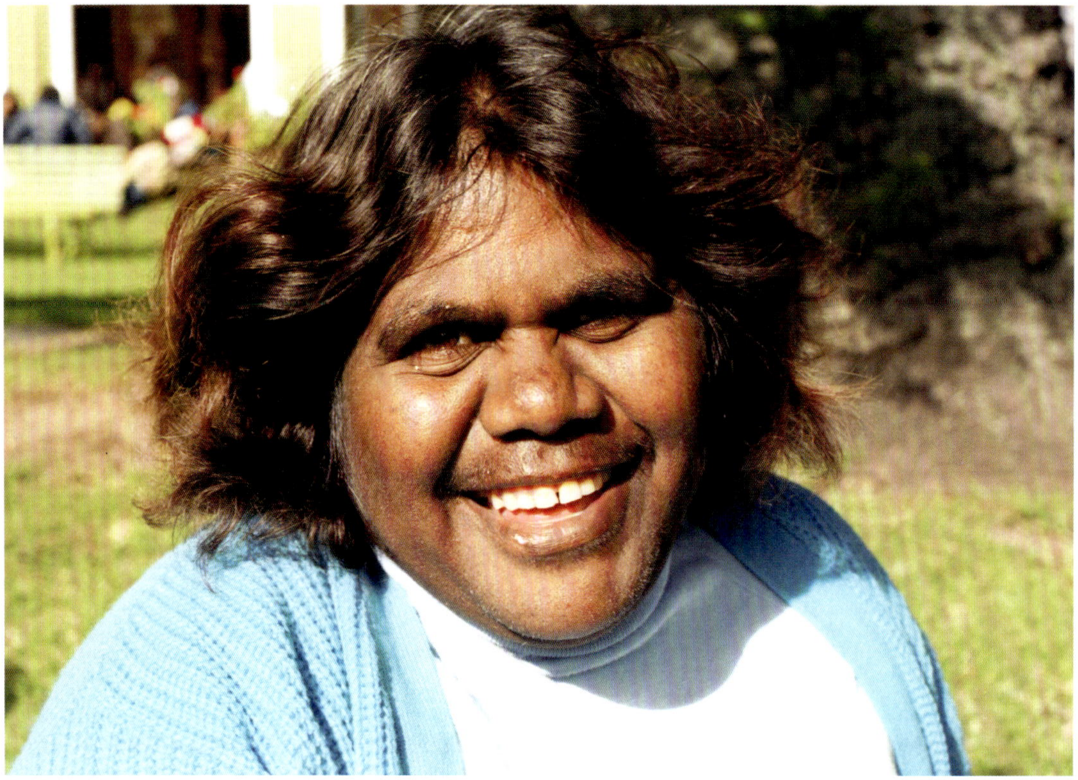

Mantatjara Wilson (1954–2009).
Photo: Collection Nganampa Health, Ara Irititja (AI-0051728)

Uwa mantaku tjitji tjuṯa fighteringi mantaku tjitji kungka tjuṯa fighteringi mantaku tjitji nyiṯayira tjuṯa, minyma tjukutjuku tjuṯa, kungkawaṟa tjuṯa, minyma puḻka tjuṯa, minyma tjukutjuku tjuṯa, pampa tjuṯa, tjilpi tjuṯa, yangapala tjuṯa. Uwankara nganaṉa tjungu tjungu alatjiṯu. Munu nganaṉa manta mantjinu panya nganampa manta nyangatja maṟu tjuṯaku iriti nguṟu.

The children fought for the land, the girls, the boys, the women, young and old, and the young and old men, all of us joined together to get the land. This is how we accomplished land rights for our people's land.[1]

Mantatjara Wilson

1 *Commemorating 10 Years of the Pitjantjatjara Land Rights Act, November 1991*, Pitjantjatjara Council & A<u>n</u>angu Pitjantjatjara, 1991, p. 11

Munula anu nganan̲a nguraritja tjut̲a Dr Coombs-alakutu munula watjan̲u, 'Ai, Dr Coombs, ngura nganampa utjunu kala uwankara pul̲kar̲a wangkanyi mantaku. Nyangatja ngura manta nganampa.' Ka tjana watjan̲u, 'Mining Company-ngku pampuntja wiya nyurampa ulpuru katutja.' Ka unngutja kul̲u ngnampa manta. Ka nganan̲a tungunpungkula pul̲kar̲a tjanala wangkangi pir̲anpa tjut̲angka nganampa mantaku. Munula nganan̲a mal̲angka waintararingu munula uwankara ngaalypa nganampa lipiringu ngananan̲anya ngaalypa utjunnyangka.

...we land owners went to Dr H.C. Coombs [politically influential supporter of Aboriginal land rights] and said, 'Dr Coombs, our land has been reduced, and we are fighting to get it back. It's our own land.' And they said, 'Mining companies cannot touch the surface of your land.' But underneath the ground is also our land. And so we relentlessly continued to speak out strongly to the Europeans for the rights to our own land. And at last we won out, and now we could take deep breaths after having been allowed only short breaths for so long.[2]

Charlie Ilyatjari

2 *Commemorating 10 Years of the Pitjantjatjara Land Rights Act, November 1991*, Pitjantjatjara Council & An̲angu Pitjantjatjara, 1991, p. 12

Charlie Ilyatjari (1928–2001) during inma at Itjinpiri the day before the handback ceremony, 3 November 1981.
Photo: Collection Jim & Shirley Downing, Ara Irititja (AI-0020798)

APY Land Rights march, Victoria Square, Adelaide, 14 February 1980.
'We were standing there in the square, just about to sing the Land Rights song. We were this small group of young women standing there ready to sing,' says Yanyi Bandicha, who in this photo is standing directly in front of the protest banner.
Photo: Collection Sandra Ken, Ara Irititja (AI-0015461)

I was working in school in Adelaide in 1980 when I heard that the people from the north-west were coming to Adelaide to fight for land rights. I started thinking: 'Yes, it is true that this land belongs to our grandfathers and grandmothers from a long time ago.' Tears were running as my thoughts went deeper and deeper. As we were singing, this song was reminding me about our people and how they used to walk from place to place and keep their sacred places without white people disturbing them. I can say now how strong we were to stand and fight to get this land back.[3]

Yanyi Bandicha (nee Baker)

3 *Commemorating 10 Years of the Pitjantjatjara Land Rights Act, November 1991*, Pitjantjatjara Council & Anangu Pitjantjatjara, 1991, pp. 20–1

We went down to Adelaide for land rights meetings, and we all camped together there, the focus being land rights. Many marvellous stories were being told, and many wonderful speeches were made. We all had a lot to think about and consider … After that, Nganyinytja went right to the centre of the meeting. She had so much confidence. We were saying, 'Hang on, you are just one woman going in to the centre of that meeting!' But she replied, 'No! I'm going in because I want to hear everything that is being said.' So in she went and she listened and gave her strong support to the government representatives who were supporting us. We all wanted to make the point that we all wanted our land. It was really important for us to be there, and they were later awarded a Member of the Order of Australia – Kawaki Punch Thompson, Donald Fraser, and my younger sister Nganyinytja.[4]

Nura Ward

4 Spoken by Nura Ward in 2010, Collection Ara Irititja (AI-0108952); first published in *Ninu, Grandmother's Law: The autobiography of Nura Nungalka Ward*, Nura Nungalka Ward, translated by Linda Rive, Magabala Books, 2018, p. 112

Nganyinytja (1929–2007): 'Nganampa Tjukurpa wiṟu alatjiṯu' ('Our Law is clear and good'). At Pitjantjatjara Council meeting in Amata, November 1980.
Photo: Collection Pitjantjatjara Council (Penny Tweedie), Aṟa Irititja (AI-0055805)

Tjunmutja Myra Watson (1927–2009) in Indulkana, next to her vehicle, c1980.
Photo: Collection Max Hart, Ara Irititja (AI-0012999)

We don't want to see the miners go in and dig up the ground that our people used to look for food on. And we will go on fighting for our land not fighting with weapons, but you know, talk and see the government, if they could give us the land and not to touch our sacred sites and that we want our children to carry on with the old ways.[5]

Tjunmutja Myra Watson

5 Spoken by Tjunmutja Myra Watson at ANZAAS (Australian and New Zealand Association for the Advancement of Science) Conference, Adelaide 1980

The Aboriginal people of this country are the only comparable indigenous people who have been given no specific rights to their own lands. The Maoris, the Eskimos [sic], the American Indians all had treaty rights and ownership and control of lands in their countries… We must, as far as we can, right the wrongs done by our forefathers.[6]

Don Dunstan, Minister for Aboriginal Affairs, SA Labor Government, 13 July 1966, in the House of Assembly: second reading of the Aboriginal Lands Trust Bill

…they were clear and adamant. They wanted a separate, new, and unique arrangement for tribal lands. To devise a framework which would, in effect, use European courts to enforce non-legal Aboriginal concepts of relationship to land was no easy task, but it was vitally important to achieve. We set up a working party of social workers and lawyers to consult and prepare a proposal.[7]

Don Dunstan, Premier of South Australia 1970–79

6 Copyright Attorney-General for and on behalf of the Crown in right of the State of South Australia

7 Don Dunstan, *Felicia: the political memoirs of Don Dunstan*, MacMillan, 1981, p. 278

Land rights consultation meeting at Iwantja/Indulkana in January 1977: Don Dunstan with (to his right) Alec Baker and Whiskey Tjukanku.
As Mumu Mike Williams says, Don Dunstan, Premier of South Australia, 'opened the door'; he led the SA Labor Government's vision for Aboriginal land rights and self-determination, and set up the Pitjantjatjara Land Rights Working Party, whose report paved the way for the *Pitjantjatjara Land Rights Act 1981*.
Photo: Collection Alan Morris, Ara Irititja (AI-0010736)

Some of the elders said, 'We need to talk to this [Liberal] government eye to eye.' Some of the women said, 'We have important sacred land also. We are coming to speak for ourselves.' So I drove a Toyota Coaster with about twenty leading ladies in it [...] 'We'll speak for ourselves,' the people said. They did so on the Victoria Racecourse site, with dramatic results. [...] the government dropped its plan to map the southern land and open it to miners. Instead they set up a consultation, which at times was a confrontation; but there was learning both ways.[8]

Reverend Jim Downing, Alice Springs Uniting Church

8 *Commemorating 10 Years of the Pitjantjatjara Land Rights Act, November 1991*, Pitjantjatjara Council & A<u>n</u>angu Pitjantjatjara, 1991, pp. 30–1

Two-day protest meeting at Victoria Park Racecourse, Adelaide, February 1980. People were demonstrating against new measures introduced by South Australia's Tonkin (Liberal) government, which had come into power in 1979, after Don Dunstan's (Labor) government. At the time, the Pitjantjatjara Land Rights Bill was still before Parliament.
Photo: Collection Pitjantjatjara Council, A<u>r</u>a Irititja (AI-0036594)

David Tonkin, Premier of South Australia, Reverend Bill Edwards (1929–2015), Arthur Richards, Punch Kawaki Thompson at Victoria Park Racecourse, Adelaide, February 1980.
Photo: Collection Pitjantjatjara Council, Ara Irititja (AI-0036589)

…the Labor Government in South Australia under Dunstan had introduced Land Rights legislation in 1965 with the setting up of the Aboriginal Lands Trust. The Whitlam Government in 1972 established a Commission to examine Land Rights in the Northern Territory. A lawyer assisting this commissioner visited Amata in 1973, as people there had association with land in the Northern Territory. This was my first experience in interpreting land rights discussions, and the response of the men at Amata was 'What is she talking about – giving us the land? It has been ours since the Tjukurpa [...].[9]

Reverend Bill Edwards, Superintendent at Ernabella Mission 1958–72

9 'Pitjantjatjara Land Rights', unpublished paper, Bill Edwards, Collection Ara Irititja (AI-0172580-015). 1991, p. 15

Men performing Ngi_ntaka Inma during the Pitjantjatjara Land Rights handback ceremony at Itjinpiri, 4 November 1981.
Photo: Collection Pitjantjatjara Council, A_ra Irititja (AI-0018518-001)

Left to right: Harold Allison (Minister for Aboriginal Affairs), Yami Lester, Phillip Toyne (lawyer), Charlie Perkins (Permanent Secretary, Department of Aboriginal Affairs) and Punch Kawaki Thompson (Chairman, Pitjantjatjara Council), at the handback ceremony, 4 November 1981, Itjinpiri.
Photo: Collection Guthrie & Irving, Ara Irititja (AI-0037965)

David Tonkin, Premier of South Australia, addressing the crowd at the Itjinpiri handback ceremony, 4 November 1981. Punch Kawaki Thompson, Chairman of the Pitjantjatjara Council at the time, is the man in the maroon shirt with yellow trim. Photo: Collection Pitjantjatjara Council, Ar̲a Irititja (AI-0018514)

An early painting by Mumu Mike depicting the Itjinpiri handback ceremony. The pink U-shape represents Mr Tonkin, holding the *Land Rights Act*, abstracted as a white rectangle. The long shape at the bottom of the canvas is the ceremonial object used for Ngi_ntaka Inma, which was performed on the day (see photo on page 158).

Land Rights Act, 2012
Mumu Mike Williams
acrylic on linen
111 x 91 cm
Private collection

Itjinpirila, 2018
At Itjinpiri, 2018

Gathering of senior men at the site of the Pitjantjatjara Land Rights handback ceremony, thirty-six and a half years after the event.

Mike Mumu Williams Palya? Uwa, nyangatjala, paint-ngka panya Tjukurpa wangkangi, panya *Land Rights Act* panya whitefellangku kuranu, ka anangu tjuta wangkantja wiyaringu. Kala nyiringka nyaangka paintangka Tjukurpa nyara palunya utinu, ngarantjaku. Ka nyaapa Tjukurpa nyara paluru anu ngura winki kutu. Kala nyangatja kuwari nyinanyi kala wangkanyi nyangatja nganana more piruku supportamilantjaku, you know, Tjukurpa nganampa. Ka nyaa, nganana paintingka tjunu, Tjukurpa pulka, ngura nganampa Tjukurpa kunpu, pulka.

Palya? Well, here we are to review the history of our *Land Rights Act*, which was the main topic of discussion many years ago. As we know, white people had made a serious problem for us, yet they'd never advised we Anangu of the situation until much later, when the story came out and we found out what had happened. The story had spread far and wide amongst our people. We began to talk amongst ourselves. We realised we needed more support to protect our Tjukurpa. This is why I have been making paintings about this history, as it is an important Tjukurpa.

Pages 162–3: Left to right: Mumu Mike Williams, Frank Young, Stanley Young, Witjiti George, Willy Muntjantji Martin, Peter Mungkuri, Taylor Cooper, Arnie Frank and Alec Baker, July 2018.

Nyangatjana walkatjunu, ngayulu Tjukurpa nyangatja walkatjura tjunu canvas nyangangka. Ka kapamantangku ngunti walytjaringanyi. Palu nganampa Tjukurpa kulu kurani. Ngunti walytjaringkula. Kana kulira walkatjunu. Ka watjanu, 'Nyaaku, nyaaku nyuntu panya mailbag-ngka walkatjunangi?'

I have written about this history on canvases. I have written about how the government believes it owns most of this land, but it doesn't. It can't. In doing so it would break the sacred Law and Tjukurpa. They think they can own it, but they can never own it. I have pondered on this and written about it. I have been asked, 'So, how come you have been painting on mailbags?'

Kana: 'Mailbag-ngka ngayulu walkatjunangi Tjukurpa panya palunya tjananya. Ngananana letter purunypa iyani. Politician panya nyakunytjaku, kutjupa tjutangku nyakunytjaku. Might be America-la nguru pitjala nyakunytjaku, 'Mulapa. Tjanampa ngura. Tjanampa Tjukurpa.' Kana nyaa walkatjunu: nganampa Tjukurpa. Nganampa manta. Nganampa Tjukurpa kunpu. Nyara palunya tjananya ngayulu walkatjunu.

My answer is this: I paint on mailbags because I want to depict our history on them. They are symbolic of letters, which we are sending out to the world. Letters for politicians to read, letters for anybody to read. People may even come from as far away as America, who may want to read my letters. The Americans may be able to read my letter and see a parallel with their country and could well say, 'It is true. This is their land. This is their culture.' This is what I depict: our Tjukurpa. Our land. Our enduring culture. This is the message I want everybody to understand.

Ka tjana riitamilani nyakula kuwari, ngura winki kutu. Ka ngananana malakungku manage *Land Rights Act* nyaratja. Ka wirunya kulini wangkara kulini manta nyangatja matjiringu munu mantjinu. Nyangangka mantjinu. Palula malangka kapamanta, kapamanta palunya katingu ngula ngura Anapalaku. Ka paluru nyangu Ananguku Tjukurpa. Miilmiilpa nyangu. Munu nyara palula nguru kutju paluru kututu alatjitu.

They'll be able to read the wording on my paintings and in my book, all over the world. We have a *Land Rights Act* here, which we manage. We had great success with our demonstrations and marches, fighting for our land, because we did eventually win the rights to our land. After one of our demonstrations, government representatives came to Ernabella to meet people and see our land and visit one of our sacred sites. They could see that our land is sacred. We proved it to them. They were prepared to give it back to us, to our heart's joy.

Ka tjana riitamilani ka kulilku, 'Uwa mulapa. Kapamanta, kunta wiya, ngunti walytjaringanyi, mineralpaku, kapiku, Tjukurpa kutjupa way, palu Tjukurpa panya ngaranyi, mineral tjuta.' Ka tjana riitamilala kulinma munta, 'Kapamanta wiya kulini!'

Anyone reading my words will understand, 'It is true. The government has no moral right to that land, its minerals, water resources and Tjukurpa cultural heritage. Anangu culture is different, and the Tjukurpa and the minerals are one and the same.' When they read these words they'll realise, 'Oh, the government has no idea!'

Because the problem pulkanya tjana wangkangi Captain Cookanya pitjangu. Munu kunyu wararakatingu tjana, and one wati. Wati kutju kunyu – tjaa kutjupangku – wangkangu, 'Australia is empty.' Ngunti wangkangu! Ngunti wangkangu, palu wiya, everything nganampa Tjukurpa everything!

Because the problem started when Captain Cook arrived and made a statement. Many people came ashore, with that one man. Apparently that man – speaking a different language – had said, 'Australia is empty.' How very wrong! He could not have been more wrong, because Aboriginal people were everywhere, and the entire continent is filled with our history and cultural heritage!

Tjaa kutjupa, nyaa panyatja, that whitefella been say – wiya, nyaa, English kutjupa tjinguru near England – watjanu, 'Wiya. Australia is empty.

He was speaking in his own language of course, I'm not sure where he was from, that white man, but he'd said – wait, of course, he spoke English, he was from England – and he said, 'No. Australia is empty.'

Palu wiya. He didn't know, paluru nganampa ngurpa, nganampa rockhole. Rockholepa nganampa Tjukurpa ngaranyi, uwankara.

He was wrong. He didn't know about us, or our rockholes. Our rockholes are all sacred Tjukurpa sites, sustaining life everywhere.

Kana walkatjura wangkangu, kapamantangku ngunti walytjaringkula, manta nganampa kurantjikitjangku Tjukurpa nganampa kurantjakitjangku. Because ngayulu walkatjunu canvas-ngka.

So I wrote this story in my paintings, to reaffirm that the government cannot own our land because if they do they'll damage our sites and our cultural heritage. We own our land and always have. Because of this, I painted all these canvases.

Witjiti George Nganana uwankara nyinangi, palu tjana kulini dingo tjuta kutju nyinanyi palku. Ngunti alatjitu. Paluru ngunti report walkatjunu letter, walkatjunu, 'Anangu wiya nyinanyi alatjitu.'

While there were untold Anangu living across the continent, they assumed only dingoes live here. How wrong they were. After that they wrote a report and posted it back, reporting, 'There are no people living here, the land is uninhabited.'

Frank Young speaking English Nyangatja, pana nyangatja, pana nyangatja, on this ground, we got the *Land Rights Act* in 1981.

On this ground here, on this very land we got the *Land Rights Act* in 1981.

We don't want any blockage in our story. We want this story to go on and come back to our kids. This *Land Rights Act* was strong when we started here. As a young man I started up talking about this *Land Rights Act*. Talking about the Law of the land, in Amata, as ten young men, we put forward Charlie Ilyatjari, when he was an old man. We started up Pitjantjatjara Council. Before APY. Pitjantjatjara Council was formed in Amata. We started up bringing in people from each community on radio call and they all came in. Nobody stopped home. They all came over there and we all camped out in the creek, and we talked about the *Land Rights Act*, and asked old people how to approach the government to talk about this Act. And we did. We did a lot of work. And more and more young people came in.

And we called in all communities, Northern Territory, Western Australia, South Australia, everywhere. All together. We fought for this country, and so we don't want to lose this country.

Mumu Mike Williams Nyaa kulinila manta nyangatja nganana mantjinu. *Land Rights Act* nyangatja.

This is what we think. This is our *Land Rights Act.*

Munu, tjukurpa palatja ngayunya nintila, ka ngayunya palu wiya, nyuntumpa tjukurpa.

I could ask you to teach me about your cultural heritage, but it would always be your cultural heritage.

Peter Mungkuri Nganana manta mantjinu. Nyangatja nganana kanyini panya panangka nganampa, nganampa alatjitu, nganampa uwankaraku. Palu kuwari problem winki tjara ka nganana uparingu. Tjutangku kurarapungu. Palu manta nyangatja nganampa alatjitu. Manta nyangangka ngayulu nyinangi alatjitu.

We got this land back. We got our own land back in order to look after it properly and continue to live on it. But nowadays there are a lot of problems and we are threatened. But this is still our land. I've lived here all my life.

Alec Baker, Frank Young, Peter Mungkuri and Witjiti George speaking together Ngura pana nyangatja ngura miilmiilpa. Ngura nganampa. Manta miilmiilpa tjara, Tjukurpa tjara alatjitu. Nganampa kamiku manta. Kamiku tjamuku manta alatjitu. Ngura miilmiilpa. Manta nganampa Tjukurpa tjara, ka nganana wirura kanyinytjikitjangku mukuringanyi.

This is a sacred land. It is our land. Our grandmothers' land. This is our grandparents' land, our grandmothers' and grandfathers'. It is sacred land. We want to keep it strong and safe.

Opposite: Mumu Mike Williams, Frank Young, Stanley Young and Witjiti George at Itjinpiri, July 2018.

Peter Mungkuri Ngura nyangatja nganana kanyinytjikitja mukuringanyi, mantangka ingkantja wiya nganana kanyintjikitja mukuringanyi nganampa ngura, tjamunya tjana purunypa kanyintjaku, tjamulu kamilu, tjana paluru wirura alatjitu kanyiningi nganmanypa, whitefella wiyangka.

We keep this land safe in the memory of our grandfathers and grandmothers. They kept it well and managed it beautifully, sustained it well as it sustained them well, in the days before white people.

Men talking together, all together, shouting together Manta nganampa. Pana nganampa. Nganana manta walytja alatjitu manta mantjinu Itjinpirila. Munu Ayers Rock. Nganana inma kantunu. Nganampa manta miilmiilpa. Nganana inma ma kantura ma kantura, pakara pakara pakara inmaku, wirunya, pukulpa pulka. Kapamantangka nganana nyinara wangkangi. Tjuta pitjangu. Nganana ara wangkangi.

Our manta. Our land. We got the land back at Itjinpiri. And at Ayers Rock [Uluru]. We danced on the land. Our sacred land. Manta miilmiilpa. We danced. It was great. The government came. We all spoke up.

Stanley Young Nganana pitjangi Pipalyatjarala nguru. Nyara palula miitingi tjaatarira wangkangi, munu Ilyatjarinya tjananya ma tjunu Amatala - miitingi nyangaku. Nganana kulira munula ngurkantanangi munuya tjilpi tjutaya ma tjunu. Ka nganana nyara palula nyinangi yangapala, ngayulu, ka nyara palula nguru Tjukurpa wangkangi, whitefella.

We were coming to the meetings from right over at Pipalyatjara. Ilyatjari and the other men organised the meeting at Amata – and the one here. We came to that meeting along with all the other old men. We were just youngfellas back then. We came here and heard the story from that whitefella.

Phillip Toyne. Paluru nyara nguru tjukurpa ma ungu. Tjukurpa ma ungu, ka [Pitjantjatjara] Council nganana ngurkantanu, Amatala. Munu tjintjirangka wangkara lipulara pitjangi.

Phillip Toyne. He came here and told us what the story was about and so we decided to set up a Pitjantjatjara Council there at Amata. We talked on the flat earth, set up the rules, got it organised.

Peter Mungkuri, Taylor Cooper, Arnie Frank and Alec Baker at Itjinpiri.

Stanley Young Arthur Richards. Paluru pitjangu. Munu nyara palula nguru pitjangu, pitjala tjukurpa nyangangka utinu. Ka winki kutju ngarangi ka tjukurpa nyara nguru katira iyaningi. Ngayuku katja pitjangu ngura nyanga kutu, Arthur Richards, munu tjukurpa palyanu nyarangka, Amatala. Number one pitjangi tjukurpa paluru pitjala pitjala pitjala Itjinpirila wirkanu. Ka winkingku kulinu miitingi kunyu ngaranyi, Itjinpirila. Phillip Toyne-nga, Arthur Richards-nga, munu Council nguru pitjangu Ilyatjarinya. Chairperson. Tjunu nyara palula putingka. Munu katira iyani. Ka tjukurpa nyanga paluru nyara nguru pitjala pakanu. Ka whitefella kutju ma pitjangi nyarangka munu pitjala nyangangka palyanu. Ka tjukurpa nyangatja lipiringu, manta nyangaku. Manta nyangaku, manta nyangatja Tjukurtjara. Ngura winki.

Arthur Richards. He came here. He came here and told us what he knew. Everybody listened and took the story back home again. Arthur Richards, my katja, was the number one leader then. We all had the meeting at Amata, and then we had many more meetings until we finally came to Itjinpiri. Everyone heard all about it and everyone came to Itjinpiri. Phillip Toyne was there, and Arthur Richards, and Charlie Ilyatjari. Chairperson. They voted him in right there in the bush. So we came here and one whitefella came here and gave us the land rights. Then the story spread far and wide. It is a sacred land.

Frank Young Before white people came and Captain Cook put his flag in the ground and said this is government ground, this is whitefella's ground – before that Anangu had their stories inside and many, many miles away – many miles away underneath. And government said they only got a piece of ground on top. Government owns inside. Because Captain Cook put his flag in and said, 'This is ours.' Anangu have been living here since before Captain Cook, and they had their stories right inside, where minerals are, where golds are, where nickels and everything are. Stories everywhere. People think, or government think, 'Oh that's nothing. That's our story.' No, it's not your story. This is Anangu story. Anangu own this land for long time. Years and years before Captain Cook. See that? That's the story.

Witjiti George Paluru tjana nyinangi alatjitu Sydneyla Melbourne-ta, everything. Uwankara, Anangu maru right through. Paluru tjana ngunti ngarala wangkangu, ngunti.

Aboriginal people were in Sydney and Melbourne and everywhere, a long time ago. There were Aboriginal people there then, right through. They said that there were no people there.

Frank Young Flag tjara paluru tjunu munu wangkangu, 'Pana nyanga unngutjanya nyangatja nganampa.' Flag wanu paluru tjarpa tjunu.

He put his flag in and said, 'This is our land now and we'll own it all, inside and out.' He did this by placing his flag there.

Frank Young Mineral, everything, kapamantaku, belong to government. Anangu tjuta miri unngutja. Munu ngananyanya katu, katutja.

Mineral, everything belong to government. Also, all the ancestral dead, buried inside the ground. While we can have what's on the surface.

Stanley Young Ka unngu nyara tjiwa winki.

Under the surface is where our flat grindstones are.

Frank Young Tjukitji kutju tjawara, tjawara tjikintjaku, that's all.

We are only allowed to dig out water soakages, to drink from them, that's all.

Willy Muntjantji Martin at Itjinpiri, July 2018, passionately speaking about the ongoing duty of the senior men, keeping the land strong for the next generation.

Willy Muntjantji Martin Nyangangkala pitjangu. Ka ngayulu Mimilila nguru pitjala nyangangkana nyangu. Ngananа matjiringu, ka tjitjingku mantjinu. Tjitji kutjungku, paper paluru mantjinu. Palunya ungu David Tonkin-tu. Tjitji nguru kanyini? Munu paluru manta nyangatja witilku. Tjilpi tjutangku wangkantja, munu wangkangu, 'Manta nyangatja nyuntu kanyinma alatjitu kunpu. Ngananа ngula wiyaringkunyangka tjilpi tjuta ngula pass away panya wiyaringanyi.' Ka ngula tjitji palurulta kanyini, malatjangku. Kunpu kanyinytjaku apu purunypa. Like apu purunypa, nyaa purunypa, kunpu ngarantjaku, uwa tjitji paluru. Paluru katantananyi? Wiya panyatja. That's Land Rights nyara paluru. Nyangatja winki. So paluru tjana matjiringu. Ka ngananа ngurpa nyinangi. Ngayulu yangupala, Mimilila nguru pitjangu. Ka ngananа tjaatarira nyanga palula nguru matjiringu, ka paluru alatji wangkangu, Premier Tonkin-tu, 'Nyuntumpa nyangatja kutju. Ka mining uwankara ngayuku. Ngayuku, Premier-ku. Ngayuku nyaratja everything, ngayuku nyaratja uwankara, mining ngayuku uwankara. But nyuntumpa nyangatja kutju. Dust alatji. Manta ulpuru. Dust.'

This is where we came to. I came here from Mimili and it was here that I witnessed the event. We all marched up, and then a child received the title deeds. A child got the document. David Tonkin presented it to him. So what will this child inherit and what will he do with it? He will hold onto this land tightly. The old men told us that they hold the land in perpetual custodianship. The old men advise, 'This land is your inheritance, so keep it strong for your own children and their descendants. We old people will pass away one day.' Then the child will take over, as a member of the younger generation. They'll keep it as strong as a stone mountain. The children will keep it as strong and eternal as the mountain ranges. Could that child break it? No. That's what our land rights are for. For here and everywhere. That's why we marched. We had no idea what was going on at first. I was just a youngfella from Mimili. But we started our struggle and we marched and demonstrated until Premier Tonkin finally said the words, 'This is your land. But the mining and everything else belongs to me. Me, as the Premier. I am in charge of mining everywhere. But this alone is yours. This dust. This dust is yours. This dust.'

Witjiti George Manta ulpuru.

Only dust.

Willy Muntjantji Martin Munu ngananaanya ungu Adelaidela, ka ngananaa anu nyara palula kutu munu matjiringu. Ngayulu kulu anu, anu nganaku Adelaide. Ka nyara palula ngananaa mantjinu.

We also received that document in Adelaide, where we'd all gone and marched and demonstrated. I went to Adelaide, too. It was there that we got the paperwork.

Alatji ka paluru wangkangu Anangu tjutaku, 'Uwa ngayulu unganyi alatjitu. Uwa, manta unganyi, palya alatjitu ngayulu unganyi Anangu tjuta because Anangu tjutaku ngura nyaratja. Uwa palya, nyara palunya ngayulu wangkanyi.'

He said to we Anangu, 'I am giving you all of your land back. Yes, we are returning your land to you because it belongs to you anyway. This is my public statement to you all.'

Munu palula nguru paluru wangkangu, 'Kunpuya kanyinma. Nyura nyangangi like eagle, walawurungku. Nyuntu kunpu kanyinma ngura nyangatja. Palu nyuntumpa kuwari nguwanpa katakatinyi, nyangatja, kuwari nyangatja katakatingulta nganampa. Nganalu, wiya kutjupa tjutangkuya nganampa kuranu. Katakatintja mulapa wiya. Ngura nyangatja ngaranyi alatjitu, nganampa.

Then after that, he said, 'But you must keep it strong. You must watch over your land as an eagle keeps an eagle eye on the land. You must keep your land strong and intact.' If anything is broken, other people would have done the breaking, not us. Our land is not broken at all. Our land remains intact and strong.

Ka nganalu kanyini Tjukurpa nyara palunya? Tjamulu. Tjamulu ngananaanya ungkukatingu kunpungku kanyinytjaku. Miri tjutangku ngananaanya Tjukurpa ungu. Wiyaringu tjutangku tjana Intalkala kuwari tjuminta ngarinyi. Nyara Mimililaya ngarinyi. Nyara paluru tjana ngananaanya Tjukurpa ungu. Munu Anapalala munu Amatala, everywhere tjuta.

So who has kept our land strong and intact? Our grandfathers. Our grandfathers and all his generations maintained our land well and handed it down through the generations to us. Our ancestors handed down the Tjukurpa to us. All our old men are now lying underneath cement slabs in Indulkana. They are lying in Mimili. They were the ones who passed on the Tjukurpa to us. They lie dead in Ernabella, Amata and everywhere on our lands. They are all dead now and lying asleep, at Amata and everywhere else.

Amatala kuwaripa tjara wangkangu. Ngayuku ngalungku pitjangu munu paluru lawyer mantjinu, Phillip Toyne. Palunya ngananaa matjiringu, munu ngananaa Land Rights nyaratja mantjinu. Nyangatja nganampa ngura. Ngananaa wiyaringanyi nyangangka. Ngananaa wiyaringanyi, ka ngarala ngaranyi alatjitu.

The meetings in Amata were relatively recent. My brother went there and he brought a lawyer with him, Phillip Toyne. After those meetings we went and marched, and we won our land rights. This is our own land after all. It will be our land even after we are gone. We will die here but our culture will carry on.

Tjinguru ngananana ilunyi, wiyaringanyi, die, ka malatja tjutangku, yangapala tjutangku kanyinytjaku. Palula nguru wangkangu, 'Nyura ngura nyangatja kanyinma and ngura pulka kutu anama.' Tjilpi tjutangku alatji wangkangu ngananananya uwankara. 'Ngura pulka atunymanama. Ngura pulka kutu katima, wati kulunypa tjuta katima, munu nintinma Tjukurpa tjuta. Tjukurpa pulka tjuta, munu pulkanya ngaranyi, miilmiilpa, nyara wilurara wanu. Nganampa ngurangka ngaranyi, ngura pulka. Munu nyangatja. Ananguku Tjukurpa. Munu nyaratja, nyara Intalka. Tjanala kutu, ngura uwankara alatjitu, Tjukurpa pulka, Yankunytjatjara, Pitjantjatjara, Ngaatjatjarra, palya?'

Let's imagine we are no longer here, we'll have passed away, fallen asleep, be dead, but the young people will take over from us in caretaking our land. Because of this fact we say, 'You must keep this land safe and go to our sacred sites to make sure they are safe.' That is what the old men said to us. 'Protect our sacred sites. Go to our important sacred sites and take the young men with you, show them around and teach them the Law. Teach them our important Tjukurpa Law that is connected to our most sacred sites that are connected to the west. Our land is full of sacred sites. Anangu have sacred Tjukurpa. Here and there at Indulkana. Travel to each site and check on it, make sure the Tjukurpa is safe for Yankunytjatjara, Pitjantjatjara and Ngaatjatjarra people, okay?'

Opposite: Granite boulders in the Everard Ranges around Mimili Community.
Photo: Rohan Thomson, 2018

A.P.Y. Kutjukurpa
Kunpu
alatjitu

APY-ku Tjukurpa Kuṉpu Alatjiṯu (Aṉangu, Pitjantjatjara, Yankunytjatjara Law and Culture is Strong), 2017
Mumu Mike Williams, Willy Muntjantji Martin, Witjiti George, Taylor Cooper
tea, ink and acrylic on paper
145 x 155 cm
Araluen Art Collection, acquired 2017
Photo: Araluen Arts Centre

Kulila. Manta munu Tjukurpa kuṉpu alatjiṯu.

Listen. The land and the Tjukurpa has its own power.

Manta Munu Tjukurpa, 2018
Mumu Mike Williams, Willy Muntjantji Martin, Sammy Dodd (spears)
synthetic polymer paint and ink on canvas mailbags and linen, with kuḻaṯa (spears) made from kuḻaṯa (spearbush), mulga, kiṯi (mulga leaf resin), maḻu pulyku (kangaroo tendon)
216 x 230 cm
Kaplan-Levi Collection

Kulila
Manta Munu
Tjukurpa
Kunpu
IS A CRIMINAL OFFENCE
PENALTIES APPLY

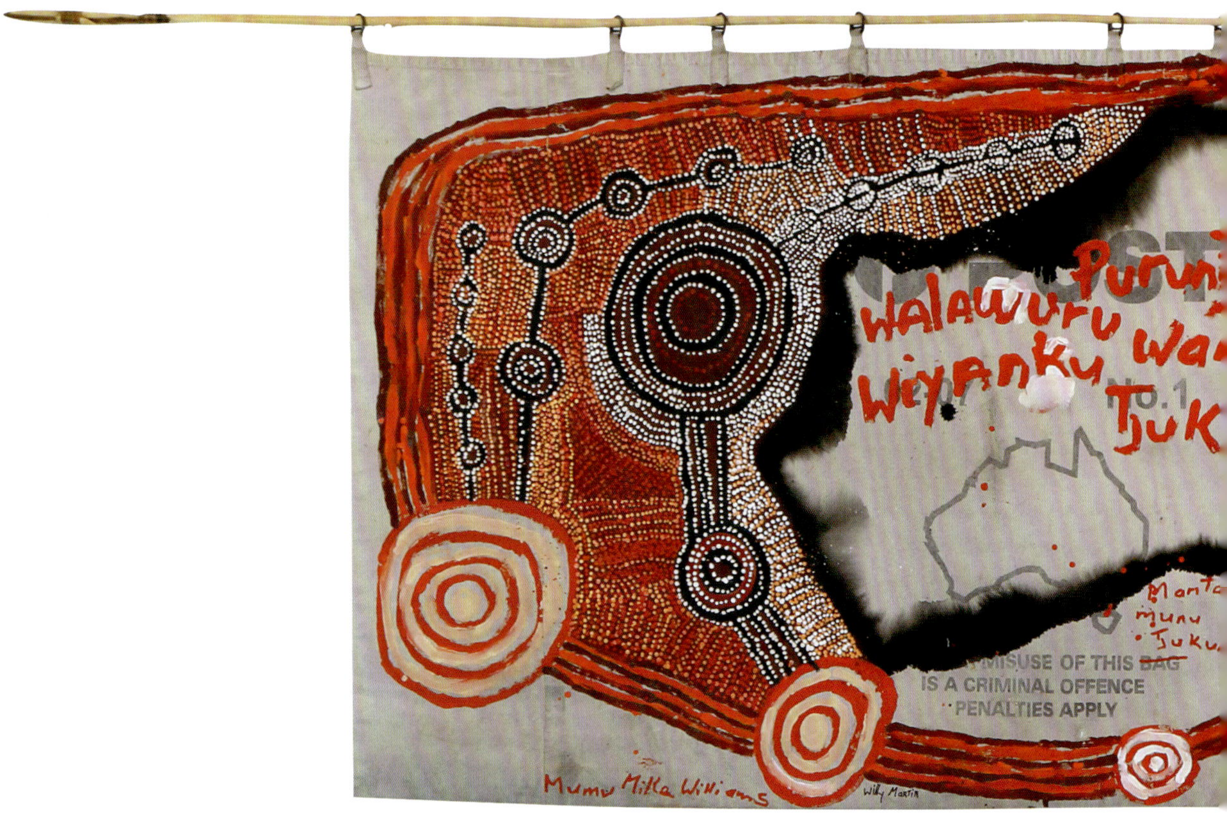
Walawuru
Wiyanku
MISUSE OF THIS BAG
IS A CRIMINAL OFFENCE
PENALTIES APPLY
Mumu Milka Williams
Willy Martin

akutja
ganampa
MunuNganampa
Manta
Willy Martin

Wal̲awuru pur̲unytju nyakunytja wiyangku wanti.
Nganampa Tjukurpa munu nganampa manta.

Stop watching us like a hawk.
This is our Tjukurpa and our land.

Theft or misuse of this land and cultural heritage is a criminal offence.
Penalties apply.

Pages 184–5: *Ngura (Country)*, 2017
Mumu Mike Williams, Willy Muntjantji Martin, Sammy Dodd (spears)
synthetic polymer paint and ink on canvas mailbags with kul̲at̲a (spear) made from spearbush, mulga, mal̲u pulyku (kangaroo tendon) and kit̲i (mulga leaf resin)
120 x 280 cm
Private collection
Photo: Outstation Gallery, Fiona Morrison

Overleaf: Looking out onto the Everard Ranges on Pitjantjatjara Country.
Photo: Rohan Thomson, 2018

Waṟu pitjantja

The way fire was returned

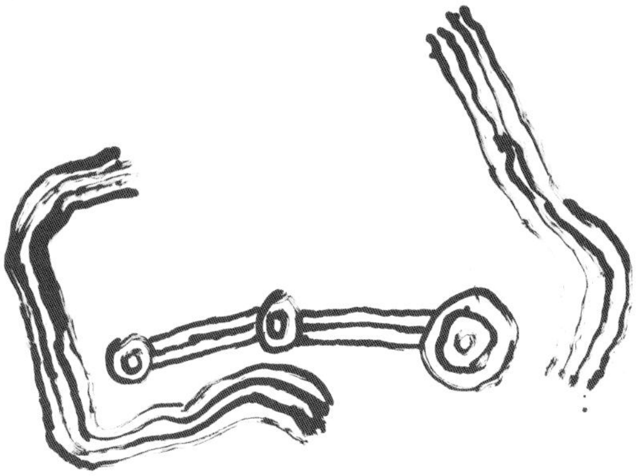

Ka wirunya ngayulu main one kulini panya waru palunya waningu Watarru-lakutu, ka tjutaringu, ngura tjutangka. Ngaltutjara.

This is one of the main traditional stories I think about the most, how the fire was brought back to Watarru and came back across the whole land. What a wonderful story.

Panya Kiparangku, waru kutitjunu. Munu paluru waru kutitjunkula anu, ngura Yalatala itingka. Munu paluru urungka tjarpangu. Tjinguru kuwari waru wiya ngarama, palu Nyiinyii wakalpai kutjarangku, wati kutjarangku, paluru pula wanara alatjitu waru pala palunya mantjinu.

The Bush Turkey stole the fire. He stole that fire and he took it all the way to a place near Yalata. He took it into the ocean. Let's say there is no fire anywhere. Then two Zebra Finch men spear him. They'd followed him and they managed to get the fire back.

Panya ngura tjutangka kutu waningu ka kuwari waru pula ngarangi. Ka pala purunypa, nganampa tjukurpa, like waru purunypa. Waru purunypa nganampa kutjantjaku tjana kulira nintiringkula tjana untjunpa nyinanytjaku, pukulpa. Ka waru wiyangka ngananana tjiturutjituru. Tjukurpa wiyangka ngananana uparinganyi.

They threw the fire across the land, and so the fire returned again. This is an example of one of our Tjukurpa stories, the way the fire was returned. This is how we would like our message to reach the world, to spread like fire burning across the land, wouldn't that be wonderful. Without fire, we are cold and miserable. Without our Tjukurpa we are weak and powerless.

Pala puṟunypa ngayulu tjukurpa ngayuku, tjananya ungu, tjukurpa *Land Rights Act*, tjukurpa maḻaku unkunytja tjananya, ungu manta wiṉki. Palu tjinguṟu kutjupangku kutitjunanyi, waṟu puṟunypa. Ka nganaṉa waṟaṟa maḻaku-ngku mantjini munu tjunanyi tjitji tjuṯaku nyakunytjaku. Panya paluṟu palya.

That is also how our own story unfolded, how our *Land Rights Act* came back to us, and the land given back to us, the rightful owners. However, we all know that our land can be stolen away from us in an instant, just like the fire was stolen. So those of us that were there to receive our land back, keep holding onto it as strongly as we can, and we are documenting it so that our children can read and learn their own history. This is a good thing.

Australia, palya?

Hetti Kemerre Perkins

Our artists invite us, and all Australians, to understand the extent of what country means for our people, revealing the nature of the relationship between community, country and culture and the attendant rights and reciprocal responsibilities that are fundamentally different to just the right to exploit the land.

Mumu Mike Williams' powerful and symbolically loaded paintings and spear installations firmly maintain the place of land rights in the Australian psyche and on the national agenda.

As he says, 'the map of Australia shows that even though I'm talking about my country, these stories are important for all Aboriginal people'. His work reflects the wonderful diversity of Aboriginal artistic traditions and shows how this cultural bedrock is so brilliantly interpreted for our contemporary world. The depiction and use of spears is central to the formidable intent of Mr Williams' works and is inspired by his brother-in-law, the legendary A<u>n</u>angu land rights activist Yami Lester, as he says on page 123 of this book: 'I listened closely to what he had to say, and I wrote down a lot about what he told me about Maralinga. I have documented his ideas about a fence made of spears, surrounding and protecting our culture and country. Imagine a fence made of spears. It would be the perfect protection.'

Like the various iterations of the Ku<u>l</u>a<u>t</u>a Tju<u>t</u>a (Many Spears) public installations and performances initiated by the APY Art Centre Collective as an ongoing inter-generational cultural maintenance project, Mr Williams' work is distinctive for its artful co-opting of Australia Post mailbags and assorted official maps, along with spears, as the support for imagery and text. Hijacking a whitefella communications system, the use of text in Mr Williams' art echoes the placards carried by protesters in the demonstrations that were central to the land rights movement. He integrates the political and cultural landscape, to answer the question 'Nyaa manta. What is land rights?' In the wake of the recent history of land rights milestones and subsequent native title legislation, Mr Williams' question is a timely one – what is land rights now?

Aboriginal guerrilla resistance was waged on many frontiers throughout the nation since the British first visited our shores, boiling over in the 1970s in a ferment of radicalism and revolutionary activism.

In the Northern Territory at Wave Hill on 23 August 1966, Vincent Lingiari led 200 Gurindji stockmen, domestic workers and their families in strike action for fair wages against the station owners, the food company Vestey Brothers. This lengthy dispute raised awareness amongst the Australian community about Indigenous land rights. The call and response mantra of 'What do we want? Land rights! When do we want them? Now!' galvanised thousands of Australians to take to the streets in support of Aboriginal claims to sovereignty. The moment, in 1975, when Vincent Lingiari received the soil of his country symbolically poured into his hands by then Prime Minister Gough Whitlam is now seared in the national consciousness through Aboriginal photographer Mervyn Bishop's iconic image and the 'de facto' land rights anthem 'From little things, big things grow' by Kev Carmody and Paul Kelly.

The land rights movement, ultimately one of self-determination, has been a battle fought not only in the bush but in the towns and cities. The erection of the Tent Embassy in Canberra was catalysed by the McMahon government's rejection of land rights following the Northern Territory Supreme Court's 1971 ruling against the Yolngu land claim in Milirrpum v Nabalco (overturned two decades later by the Mabo v Queensland decision). Our people united to take the fight from the political fringes to the doorstep of the nation's political heartland. Originally no more than a humble beach umbrella planted on the lawns of (Old) Parliament House replete with the newly created Aboriginal flag, the Tent Embassy became a rallying point for a people who had become strangers in our own land and a thorn in the side of the federal government:

...every day they've got to remember the blacks are there, the blacks are there, the blacks are there and they're not going to go away and that made them think and it disturbed them. They couldn't sleep at night... And they wanted us all to go away and disappear and we weren't going to do that.[1]

On the crest of public outcry, the Aboriginal Land Rights (Northern Territory) Act was passed with historic bipartisan support in December 1976. From this, four land councils, including the Northern Land Council (NLC) and Central Land Council (CLC), were established. In the same year, tri-state desert communities traversing South Australia, Western Australia and the Northern Territory formed the Pitjantjatjara Council. In their first letter to the South Australian Government asserting their traditional territorial rights, they stated 'we have one law and we are one, no matter where we come from, we have this one law and we've got one law all the time'.[2] The *Pitjantjatjara Land Rights Act* (latterly *A<u>n</u>angu Pitjantjatjara Yankunytjatjara Land Rights Act* or *APYLRA*) was passed by the South Australian Government in 1981. This landmark legislation granted A<u>n</u>angu *full powers to manage and control access to the lands, to share control of mining with the government and receive a third of the royalties from mineral extraction. The APYLRA marked the single biggest return of land to Indigenous Australians and was 'the first negotiated land rights settlement in Australia'.* [3]

Whether it's the Yirrkala Bark Petition or the Barunga Statement, the painting-up to dance for country to evidence land claims, the triumphs and tragedy of Albert Namatjira's life, the crafting and carrying of placards in street demonstrations, the

1 'Australian Biography: Charles Perkins' interview conducted by Robin Hughes on 6 May 1998, Tape 6, courtesy Film Australia Collection, National Film and Sound Archive

2 Arthur Richards, Secretary of Pitjantjatjara Council, 1976, cited in *Commemorating 10 Years of the Pitjantjatjara Land Rights Act*, Pitjantjatjara Council & A<u>n</u>angu Pitjantjatjara, 1991, p. 6

3 'Returning Parna Wiru: Restitution of the Maralinga Lands to Traditional Owners in South Australia' by Odette Mazel, p. 167 in *Settling with Indigenous People: Modern treaty and agreement-making*, Marcia Langton (ed.), Federation Press, 2006; Nicolas Peterson in *Aboriginal land rights: a handbook*, Nicolas Peterson (ed.), Canberra: Institute of Aboriginal Studies, 1981, pp.115–27

outstation move back to country following the *NT Land Rights Act* and the subsequent flourishing of community art centres, Michael Jagamara Nelson's mosaic in the Parliament House forecourt in Canberra, the making of artworks that creatively reiterate connection to country through the Dreamings, or Richard Bell's *Embassy* (2013) – a contemporary iteration of the Tent Embassy – Aboriginal artists continue to be the visionary voice for our people and their message is one that cannot and should not be ignored. Our artists tell us the answer to 'what is land rights?'. The fundamental right that land rights recognises is the right to a future for all our people in Australia.

In 2016 artists from communities throughout Central Australia were invited to reflect on the national significance of land rights in Australia's history. At the opening of the *Our Land Our Life Our Future* exhibition at Tangentyere Artists Gallery in Alice Springs, marking fifty years since the Wave Hill Walk-off and forty years of land rights, Mr David Frank, from Indulkana Community on the APY Lands, was awarded the Central Land Council Delegates' Choice Award for his painting *Our Future*. In bringing together the work of artists from across Central Australia, the CLC and Desart emphatically showed that this is Aboriginal land – always was, always will be. Mr Frank was one of many artists, including Vincent Namatjira and Robert Fielding, who revisited the moment in 1975 when Walk Off leader Vincent Lingiari received the soil from then Prime Minister Whitlam.

Mumu Mike Williams' painting for this historic anniversary exhibition depicts the far-reaching embrace of the Minyma Kutjara embedded within twinned maps of Australia, flanked by two kuḻaṯa (spears). His art shows that land rights have given us a future; one that has been handed to us by our old people, one that is animated by the hands of our artists. Now the future is in *our* hands and we are in good hands with Mr Williams. Like a kuḻaṯa, his message is straight and true, and one all Australians need to hear, palya?

October 2018

Our Future, 2016
David Frank
acrylic on linen
36 x 51 cm
Photo: Courtesy the artist and Iwantja Arts

Nyaa manta?
Wiya.
Wati tjilpi tjut̲aku
munu minyma tjut̲aku,
panya manta ngar̲anyi nyangangka
winkitja ngar̲anyi nyangangka.
Wati tjilpi tjut̲aku munu
minyma pampa tjut̲aku kul̲u.
Kulinma. Tit̲utjarangku
manta nyangatja tjukurtjara
nganampa altatjit̲u.
Kulini nyura?

What is land?
No.
It belongs to the old men and the old women.
Understand that this whole continent is sacred land,
belonging to the senior men and women.
Listen. This whole continent is filled with the power of the Dreaming.
It is our land.
Do you understand me?

Overleaf: *Nyaa Manta,* 2016
Mumu Mike Williams, Sammy Dodd (spears)
tea, ink, chalk pastel on paper, framed by kul̲at̲a (spears)
200 x 150 cm

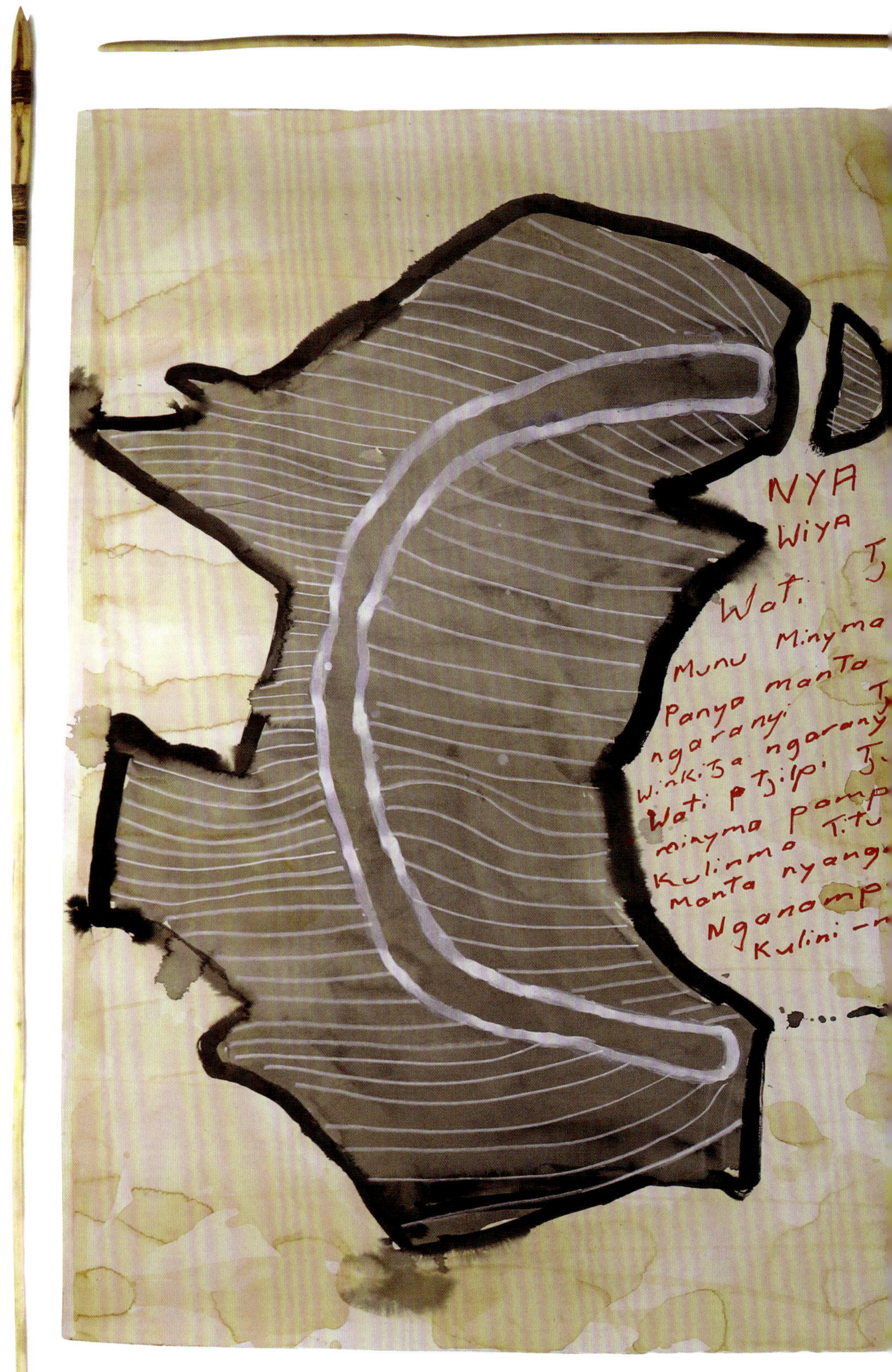
NYA
Wiya
Wat.
Munu Minyma
Panya manta
ngaranyi
Kulinma
Kulini

Milmilpa
Mumu Mike Williams

Contributors

Mumu Mike Williams

b. 1952, near Pukatja/Ernabella, South Australia
d. 2019
Pitjantjatjara

Mumu Mike Williams was born between Kenmore Park and Pukatja. He learnt to read and write in Pitjantjatjara and English at the Ernabella Mission School, before working as a stockman on cattle stations. In the 1970s he travelled the world as a pastor and orator, before returning to the APY Lands to build houses in his home community of Ernabella.

Mr Williams was active in the APY Land Rights movement that led to the signing of the *Pitjantjatjara Land Rights Act* in 1981 and the return of land to Anangu. He was also a renowned ngangkari (traditional healer), pastor of the Mimili Community church, and political activist. Mr Williams became a celebrated senior artist and writer, addressing issues including governance, sustainable land management, the protection of sacred heritage sites, and the rights of traditional owners. Creating this book was Mr Williams' long-held dream. He passed away soon after approving the final pages.

Represented by Mimili Maku Arts
Photo: Rohan Thomson

Sammy Dodd

b. 1946, near Kenmore, South Australia
Pitjantjatjara

Sammy Dodd was born to an Afghani/Arabana father and a Pitjantjatjara mother near Kenmore on the APY Lands in South Australia. As a young boy he travelled extensively with his father's camel wagon, out past his mother's country of Watarru and all the way east to Aputula/Finke and Oodnadatta. Sammy attributes his legendary craftsmanship and knowledge of kulata (spears) to this period of his life, when he sat and watched the old men craft kulata and miru (spear throwers) for hunting. After the closure of Everard Park Station near Mimili, he began working in land management, teaching youngfellas about country and kulata.

Represented by Mimili Maku Arts
Photo: Ben Searcy

Willy Muntjantji Martin

b. 1950, Pukatja/Ernabella, South Australia
d. 2018
Pitjantjatjara

Mr Martin was a respected senior man and community leader in Mimili Community. Born around Pukatja, he started working on sheep stations at a young age, and only moved to Mimili when he met his wife Judy. After working in different roles within community, Mr Martin became one of the founding members of the art centre, working prolifically until the day of his passing. Mr Martin painted Tjukurpa from around Piltati, passed on to him by the men in his family. The strong body of work he leaves behind shows his commitment to passing this knowledge on to the next generation: 'It's important that we hold our culture, our stories, our connection to country strong for maḻatja-maḻatja (future generations) – that's why I make paintings.'

Represented by Mimili Maku Arts
Photo: Mimili Maku Arts

Frank Young

b. 1949, near Atuti, South Australia
Pitjantjatjara

Frank Young is a senior Law man on the APY Lands. He is Chairman of the APY Council, a long-time Director of Tjala Arts and former chairperson of the Watarru and Amata communities. A longstanding advocate for A<u>n</u>angu land rights, he worked with senior men in the 1970s/1980s land rights movement. He is dedicated to maintaining strong A<u>n</u>angu culture, particularly through involvement in the arts and Indigenous-owned and run art centres. Alongside working with his family on collaborative paintings and projects, Frank has been heavily involved in the Kuḻaṯa Tjuṯa Project since its inception, passing on knowledge of spear-making to his grandsons and other young men. He was a key contributor to the men's collaborative painting *Kuḻaṯangku angakanyini manta munu Tjukurpa (Country and Culture will be protected by spears)* commissioned by the Australian War Memorial, Canberra, in 2017.

Represented by Tjala Arts
Photo: Rohan Thomson

Peter Mungkuri

b. 1946, near Granite Downs, South Australia
Yankunytjatjara

Peter Mungkuri was born in the bush near Lambina/Granite Downs and lived a traditional life with his parents, three brothers and many sisters. During his early childhood the cattle stations at Mimili and Granite Downs were established, and as a young man he worked for the small Mimili community, watering the trees and establishing a bush garden. Peter never attended school, instead learning about the land and his culture from his parents and family. As a young man he worked as a cook at a neighbouring cattle station and began riding their horses, going on to become a highly skilled horseman. As a stockman he travelled on horseback between Mimili and Oodnadatta, Kenmore Park and Aputula/Finke, mustering cattle and droving for weeks on end alongside his friends (and future painting colleagues) Alec Baker and Whiskey Tjukanku. Peter's paintings express his extensive knowledge of country and Anangu culture, and reflect his experiences of working the land. He won the prestigious Hadley's Art Prize in 2017.

Represented by Iwantja Arts
Photo: Rohan Thomson

Alec Baker

b. 1932, Shirley Well, South Australia
Pitjantjatjara, Yankunytjatjara

Alec Baker is an elder and respected tjilpi in Indulkana. He lived a traditional way of life with his family in the rugged bushland and desert areas of the eastern Yankunytjatjara region of the APY Lands. Today he is recognised as a respected stockman, cultural Law man and contemporary artist. He moved to Iwantja/Indulkana community in the early 1960s where he was the first senior desert man to begin painting, later travelling with fellow artist Sadie Singer to Adelaide to petition the South Australian Government to establish Iwantja Arts. The topographic map-like imagery in his detailed paintings and drawings reflects his knowledge of the land and his exceptional bush skills, acquired during a lifetime of experience of living and growing with the land.

Represented by Iwantja Arts
Photo: Rohan Thomson

Witjiti George

b. 1938, Granite Downs, South Australia
Pitjantjatjara, Yankunytjatjara

Witjiti George holds extensive cultural knowledge and is a senior artist and elder. He was born at Lambina/Granite Downs, a cattle station in the far north of South Australia. His father was from Iltur (Coffin Hill), a site associated with men's ceremony, and his mother's country is Piltati in the Mann Ranges. Due to an extended drought, his family were forced to travel east to the Central Australia Railway. It was at this time he attended primary school at Oodnadatta before moving to Pukatja/Ernabella and finally to Kaltjiti/Fregon to work in the cattle industry. With his wife Tjangili, Witjiti established the small community of Mulga Bore, east of Kaltjiti.

Represented by Kaltjiti Arts
Photo: Rohan Thomson

Taylor Cooper

b. 1940, Malara, near Pipalyatjara, South Australia
Pitjantjatjara

Taylor Cooper is an important senior artist and a recognised custodian of traditional Law and culture. He was born at Malara, a waterhole near Pipalyatjara. His father was from Pipalyatjara and his mother from Iltur (Coffin Hill), a site associated with traditional men's ceremony. Malara is the place of the Wanampi Tjukurpa (Rainbow Serpent Dreaming) in the far west of the APY Lands, which often features in Taylor's works. An expert craftsman, he continues to make kulata (spears) and kulata miru (spear throwers).

Represented by Kaltjiti Arts
Photo: Rohan Thomson

Arnie Frank

b. 1960, Yanyarinyi, near Kenmore Park Station, South Australia
Pitjantjatjara

Arnie has lived in Fregon community since it became a cattle station in 1961. His father was one of the main cattlemen. He is a senior lawman, artist and ngangkaṟi (traditional healer), and has strong connections all across the APY Lands. Arnie is passionate about passing his knowledge of Tjukurpa, which informs his skills as ngangkaṟi, on to the next generation. He often refers to kililpi (stars), whose spirit is one of the most important teachers for ngangkaṟi.

Represented by Kaltjiti Arts
Photo: Kaltjiti Arts

Stanley Young

b. 1949, near Irrunytju, South Australia
Pitjantjatjara

Stanley grew up in the bush and travelled with his family around the areas of Irrunytju and Pipalyatjara. As a young boy he attended Ernabella Mission School but returned to Pipalyatjara as a man, where he taught whitefellas Pitjantjatjara.

Stanley has had many jobs in his life including geologist, rubbish truck driver and cattleman, working at the Amata Station and Mulga Park Station. Once he rode from Alice Springs to Kalka bareback in a race with a friend. He now lives between Amata and Kalka Community, as a senior lawman, respected elder and celebrated dancer. He also works in the camel business.

Photo: Mimili Maku Arts

Hetti Kemerre Perkins

b. 1965, Sydney

Curator, writer and presenter Hetti Perkins is a member of the Arrernte and Kalkadoon Aboriginal communities. Her father, Charlie Perkins, was present at the APY handback ceremony at Itjinpiri. Hetti was senior curator of Aboriginal and Torres Strait Islander art at the Art Gallery of New South Wales in Sydney. She is the recipient of the University of NSW Alumni Award 2017 Arts and Culture and the International Council of Museums (ICOM) Australia 2017 Award. In 2018 she was also awarded an Australia Council Fellowship.

Photo: Susie Hagon, courtesy Hibiscus Films

Linda Rive

b. 1954, Cornwall, UK

Linda Rive has been working with Western Desert speaking people since the late 1970s and is a Pitjantjatjara–Yankunytjatjara–English interpreter and translator. She is known and trusted by Anangu across the tri-state region APY Lands and beyond. Her wide-ranging work in the region as an interpreter/ translator has included tourism, national parks and the environment, arts and culture, radio, film and publications. She works in an ongoing capacity with the NPY Women's Council, Tjanpi Desert Weavers, the Ngangkari Traditional Healers, and the APY Art Centre Collective, which includes Mimili Maku Arts. She is a cultural adviser to researchers, and somehow fits this in around her regular day job with Ara Irititja as an oral historian and digital archivist.

Photo: courtesy Linda Rive

Glossary

The English definitions of Pitjantjatjara words in this list relate primarily to how they are used in this book. We use the spelling convention of retroflexes (underlining) in the Pitjantjatjara text, to distinguish the different r-like sounds common to Pitjantjatjara and Yankunytjatjara. This convention is not always used by fluent speakers of the languages such as Mumu Mike Williams, for whom it is largely superfluous.

aalpiri	early morning speeches and instructions, expressing views on public matters and venting grievances
Anangu	people of the Western Desert language groups
APY Lands	region in the far north-west of South Australia, comprising the traditional lands of Pitjantjatjara, Yankunytjatjara and Ngaanyatjarra people across more than 103 000 square kilometres
The Bungalow	children's institution established by the Australian Government in 1914 in Alice Springs, NT; children of mixed descent in the Central Australian region were taken from their parents by the government and forced to live here and attend school
Emu Field	site in the southern APY Lands where nuclear bomb tests were conducted by the British Government in October 1953, which exposed the country and its people to radiation fallout
inma	ceremony incorporating singing and dancing; song
Inturtjanu	Mumu Mike Williams' birthplace
irati	poison, nuclear radiation, nuclear fallout
irkapiri	close relatives of a boy passing through man-making ceremonies; it excludes his brothers
karu	watercourse
kiti	bush glue, often made from spinifex resin; Sammy Dodd instead makes it from the leaves of a species of mulga *(Acacia Minyura)*
kulata	spear, spearbush
kunpu	strong
malu pulyku	kangaroo tendon
manta	country, place, land, ground, earth
Maralinga	a term referring to numerous sites used between 1956 and 1963 for seven British atomic bomb tests and hundreds of smaller trials, supported by the Australian Government

Minyma Kutjara ‘Two Women’ – this is Mumu Mike Williams’ Tjukurpa; he tells an outline of the story on page 8 and page 50

Ngaatjatjarra a dialect of the Western Desert language, spoken to the west of Pitjantjatjara country

ngaltutjara bless; poor thing

ngangkari traditional healer

ngura country, place, home

nyiinka boy at the stage of seclusion preceding initiation as a man; a nyiinka must avoid contact with women and girls and all but a small set of adult men during this time, and traditionally had to prove his hunting skills, self-reliance and discipline

palya good, okay, hello, bye

pampa senior woman

Pitjantjatjara a dialect of the Western Desert language

punu wood, timber, tree

tawara segregated young men’s camp, relating to a stage shortly after initiation into manhood

tjilpi senior man

Tjukurpa Tjukurpa is an ongoing, eternal, life-giving transformative power that accounts for every aspect of existence. It also refers to the creation ancestors, the country where spirit resides, and to ceremonial designs and songs that represent those beings. The Law that governs daily and ceremonial life emanates from Tjukurpa. There is no word in English that properly conveys the complex concept of Tjukurpa, which is sometimes simplified to ‘Dreaming’.

uwa yes

wata spearhead

wiltja shade shelter

wiya no

Yankunytjatjara a dialect of the Western Desert language, spoken to the east of Pitjantjatjara country

List of works

The artworks of Mumu Mike Williams and his collaborators included in this book are listed here chronologically, together with Mimili Maku Arts' catalogue number for each work. Full captions and most credits appear with the images at the referenced page numbers. Any others are listed in the additional photo credits section.

The transcriber of Mumu's artwork texts has chosen to correct any spelling errors, so that the transcriptions are spelt correctly according to conventions established when a writing system for Pitjantjatjara was standardised. Mumu does not use retroflexes. The transcriber has added retroflexes. In the main body of the text, retroflexes are also included.

Land Rights Act
no. 53–2012
p. 161

Tjilpi munu pampangku Tjukurpa kunpu kanyintjaku (It's the senior men and senior women who keep the Law strong)
no. 84–16
p. 59

Tjilpi munu pampangku Tjukurpa kunpu kanyintjaku (It's the senior men and senior women who keep the Law strong)
no. 85–16
p. 63

Tjilpi munu pampangku Tjukurpa kunpu kanyintjaku (It's the senior men and senior women who keep the Law strong)
no. 86–16
p. 60

Tjilpi munu pampangku Tjukurpa kunpu kanyintjaku (It's the senior men and senior women who keep the Law strong)
no. 87–16
p. 64

Irati (Poison) Story
no. 88–16
p. 132

Kulatangku
no. 151–16
pp. 126–7

Iyukuta Tjukurpa
no. 152–16
p. 67

Nyaa Manta
no. 170–16
pp. 198–9

Australia-ku Tjukurpa
no. 221–16
p. 97

Kulinma Tjukurpa Kunpu Nyangatja
no. 275–16
pp. 70–1

Postbag Painting
no. 428–16
p. 110

APY-ku Tjukurpa Kunpu Alatjitu (Anangu, Pitjantjatjara, Yankunytjatjara Law and Culture is Strong)
no. 98–17
p. 180

Mapa Wiya
no. 177–17
p. 82

Ngura (Country)
no. 208–17
p. 102

Ngura (Country)
no. 260–17
p. 105

Postbag Painting
no. 318–17
p. 109

Ngura (Country)
no. 320–17
pp. 114–15

Tjukurpa Kuṉpu (Strong Law and Culture)
no. 391–17
p. 85

Ngura (Country)
no. 527–17
pp. 184–5

Postbag Painting
no. 528–17
p. 98

Postbag Painting
no. 542–17
p. 101

Iyukuḻa Tjukurpa
no. 93–18
p. 113

Kulilaya munuya nitiriwa (Listen and learn from us)
no. 109–18
pp. 46–7

Pina Aḻangku
no. 189–18
p. 106

Manta Munu Tjukurpa
no. 252–18
p. 183

Kamantaku Tjukurpa wiya (The government doesn't have Tjukurpa)
no. 439–18
Gatefold

Additional photo credits

Photos have been credited within the pages to this book, apart from the following: p. iv: Rhett Hammerton; pp. vi–vii: Mimili Maku Arts; p. x: Rohan Thomspon, 2017; p. 29: Mimili Maku Arts, Jackson Lee; p. 48: Mimili Maku Arts, Angus Webb; p. 57: Mimili Maku Arts; pp. 70–1: Mimili Maku Arts, p. 72: Mimili Maku Arts; p. 77: Mimili Maku Arts; p. 82: Mimili Maku Arts; p. 85: Mimili Maku Arts; pp. 86–7: Mimili Maku Arts, Angus Webb; p. 88: Rhett Hammerton; p. 91: Mimili Maku Arts, Angus Webb; pp. 94–5: Mimili Maku Arts, Angus Webb; p. 106: Mimili Maku Arts; p. 110: Mimili Maku Arts; p. 116–17: Mimili Maku Arts, Angus Webb; p. 119: Mimili Maku Arts, Angus Webb; p. 162–3: Mimili Maku Arts, Angus Webb; p. 168: Mimili Maku Arts, Angus Webb; p. 171: Mimili Maku Arts, Angus Webb; p. 174: Mimili Maku Arts, Angus Webb; p. 183: Mimili Maku Arts; p. 197: Mimili Maku Arts; p. 214: Rhett Hammerton.

Acknowledgements

This book was initiated and led by Mumu Mike Williams. All content was audio-recorded in the author's first language, Pitjantjatjara. All translations were approved by the author. The project was managed as part of the Mimili Maku Arts program with art centre staff Anna Wattler and Angus Webb.

From Mumu Mike Williams

Imagine a kulata (spear). A big storm throws the kulata off track. It falls. But the spear is strong: the kiti is hard, the malu pulyku is firm, the kata is sharp. The kulata never breaks. It will always be picked up again, thrown again.

Now, after reading this book you know that I like to speak in pictures. When I talk about the kulata, I talk about culture, community, Tjukurpa. When I talk about the storm, I talk about government, policies, mining companies. They may try to throw us off track, but they can never stop us. Our culture is strong like a kulata, and it will always be. Through our art centres, we Anangu share our stories, but we also make real changes, when government fails. We have strong leaders on the APY Lands, but we have seen too many of them pass on in the past twelve months. I trust in the children growing up now to follow in our footsteps. But they have to learn, be proud of their culture, of the knowledge their elders hold. That's why I wrote this book. I hope that soon all children in Australia can learn about the story of APY Land Rights, about the way their ancestors fought for the land, and about the way art can move mountains.

I want to thank everyone who has made this book possible, first and foremost my friends at Mimili Maku Arts. Without the art centre this book would not have come into being.

I also want to thank my friends at the APY Art Centre Collective, and at all art centres on the lands. It is with you, that we can keep our culture strong and share it with the world.

To Shaun Berg, who has shared his legal expertise with me on more than one occasion.

To my dear friend Frank Young, whose leadership always gives me hope and who has supported me throughout the process of writing this book.

To Sammy Dodd, who has been like a brother to me. I am very happy you decided to contribute to my book.

To my long-term collaborator and friend Willy Muntjantji Martin. You were a strong leader for the APY Lands, and it was with greatest sadness I had to see you go before me. You knew, it was your time, and we will always remember you for your kindness.

To my brother Yami Lester, who has left a strong legacy and who has fought for Anangu rights all his life.

To my lifelong friend George Kenmore, who has more than once saved my life.

To my wife Tuppy Goodwin, who has patiently stayed by my side during illness, and who continues to support me daily.

To my family and friends in Pukatja, in particular to my sister Atipalku, who was there for so many memories captured in this book.

To my granddaughters Jasmin and Kishana. You are the future.

13 March 2019

From Mimili Maku Arts

Books are a great collaborative effort that bring together many talents. Mimili Maku Arts would like to thank all supporters who have generously given their time to this project.

To Karin Riederer, for connecting the dots and being the most thorough, professional yet approachable editor one could wish for. This project has relied on your thoughtful scholarly support.

To Linda Rive, who with her unerring linguistic talent and expertise for Pitjantjatjara always found the right words. Without your passionate contribution, this book would be unthinkable.

To all contributors to the Aṟa Irititja archive, who have been repatriating images and cultural materials since 1994. Being accountable to Aṉangu ways of knowing and sharing information, the archive holds great importance to Aṉangu across the lands and has been instrumental in the research for this book.

To Hetti Kemerre Perkins, for her contribution to the book. Her sustained engagement with Mr Williams' artistic practice, alongside her lived experience of land rights protests, has resulted in an essay rich with insights and contexts.

We especially acknowledge the galleries and institutions that have worked alongside us for a long time, supporting the art centre and its artists.

We thank the funding bodies for their vision, trust and commitment to this project; in particular the Gordon Darling Foundation and the Australian Government's Indigenous Languages and Arts (ILA) program.

Thank you to the Indigenous Visual Arts Industry Support (IVAIS) for your ongoing funding, enabling art centres to operate as some of the only non-government income opportunities for Aṉangu in remote communities.

This book is the first of its kind and we hope it will encourage many more artists from the APY Lands and beyond to tell their story, write in language, and celebrate the incredibly resilient life stories they have.

Mr Williams was an extraordinary artist and thinker, a fiercely resilient leader with ardent passion, devotion and creativity. Despite the fact that he spent much of the past twelve months in hospital, he continued to fervently work on his biggest projects to date. His resolute desire to be heard, combined with his unequalled imagination and vision, resulted in the book at hand. *Kulinmaya!* grew beyond anyone's expectations, including his. He was immensely proud of the result. Sadly, Mr Williams passed away shortly after approving the final pages. While he won't be among us to witness its publication, his powerful voice and legacy remain for us to heed.

We cannot wait for *Kulinmaya!* to be read by children and adults across the country. We all have some lessons to learn from a very wise tjilpi.

17 March 2019

Index

Page numbers in *italics* refer to captions of photographs.

aa<u>l</u>piri 40, 80–1
Aboriginal Land Rights (Northern Territory) Act 1976 194
Aboriginal Lands Trust 157
Allison, Harold *159*
Amata 27, 138, *139*, *149*, 157, 168, 170-172, 177
A<u>n</u>angu people *14*, *19*, 27, 122, *139*, 166, 172, 194
A<u>n</u>angu Pitjantjatjara Yankunytjatjara (APY) Lands viii, *ix*
APY Art Centre Collective 192
Ayers Rock (Ulu<u>r</u>u) 141, 170

Baker, Alec *131*, *153*, *164*, 169, *171*, 202
Baker, Ivan *139*
Bandicha, Yanyi 28, *146*, 147
Barunga Statement 194
Bell, Richard 195
Bishop, Mervyn 193
brickmaking 21, *23*
bush foods 13, 129
Bush Turkey 190

Carmody, Kev 193
Central Land Council 194
Cook, James 166–7, 172
Coombs, Dr H.C. 144
Cooper, Taylor *123*, *164*, *171*, 203

dancing 26, *158*
Davis, Bill *29*
dingo scalps 14, *19*
Dodd, Sammy 52, *53*, 56–7, *57*, 200
Downing, Reverend Jim 154
Dunstan, Don 152, *153*, *155*, 157

Edwards, Reverend Bill *156*, 157
Edwards, Tjilari 5, *14*
elders 1, 21, 41, 69, 130, *131*, 154, 202–4
Emu Field *131*, 133
Ernabella 4, 6, 8–9, *13*, *14*, 21, *23*, 128, 140, 166, 177
Ernabella Mission *5*, *6*, 157
Ernabella School *11*
Everard Ranges *178*, *187*

Fielding, Robert 195
fire, return of 190–1
Frank, Arnie *164*, *171*, 204
Frank, David *131*, 195
Fraser, Donald 148
Fregon 27

George, Nyunutja *19*
George, Witjiti *123*, *164*, 167, 169, *169*, 173, 176, 203
government 44, 58, 65–6, 69, 83, 138, 140, 165–8, 170, 172–3, 193–4
Gurindji stockmen 193

Ilyatjari, Charlie 144, *145*, 168, 170, 172
Indulkana 177–8
initiation 24–6
Inturtjanu 4, 8–9, *9*, 66
Itjinpiri 138–88, *139*, *145*, *158–61*, *169*, *171*, *174*
Iyukuta 8, 66

karu 33
Kelly, Paul 193
Ken, Sandra *29*
ku<u>l</u>a<u>t</u>a *53*, 56–7, 122–7, 134–5
Ku<u>l</u>a<u>t</u>a Tju<u>t</u>a (Many Spears) project *123*, *131*, 192

land rights 44, 51, 83, 96, 138–88, *145*, *155*, 193–5
Land Rights Acts, *see Aboriginal Land Rights (Northern Territory) Act 1976*; *Pitjantjatjara Land Rights Act 1981*
Land Rights song 28, *29*, *146*
Lennon, Albert 141
Lester, Yami 123, 129, 130, *131*, *159*, 192
letter-writing 90, 165
Lingiari, Vincent 193, 195
Lyons, Mildred Yangkuyi *139*

Mabo High Court decision 193
mailbags 90–118, 165
Many Spears project *123*, *131*, 192
Maralinga 123, 128–9, *131*, 133
Martin, Willy Muntjantji *123*, *164*, *174*, 175–8, 201
Mazel, Odette 194
McMahon government 193
memory 76
Mimili 128, 138, 177
Mimili Maku Arts viii, 92
mining companies 69, 83, 144, 151, 175, 194
Minyma Kutjara (Two Women) 8, 50, 195
Mungkuri, Peter *164*, 169–70, *171*, 202

Namatjira, Albert 194
Namatjira, Vincent 195
Nelson, Michael Jagamara 195
Ngaatjatjarra people 178
Nganyinytja 148, *149*
Ngintaka Inma *158*, 161
Nicholson, Nancy 6, 10, *11*
Northern Land Council 194
Northern Territory, land rights in 157
nuclear testing 128–9, 133
nuclear waste 65

Our Land Our Life Our Future exhibition 195

painting 50–71, 78
Perkins, Charlie *159*, 194
Perkins, Hetti Kemerre 192–5, 205
Peterson, Nicholas 194
Pitjantjara Council 168, 171, 194
Pitjantjatjara Council meeting *139*, *149*
Pitjantjatjara Land Rights Act 1981 viii, 28, 44, 51–2, 122, *153*, *161*, 164, 166–9, 191, 194
Pitjantjatjara Land Rights Bill *155*
Pitjantjatjara Land Rights handback ceremony *139*, *145*, *158–61*, 164
Pitjantjatjara Land Rights Working Party *153*
Pitjantjatjara language 6, 10–11
Pitjantjatjara people 178
Pompey, Jimmy *131*
Pukatja 50

radio 130
Richards, Arthur *156*, 172, 194
Rive, Linda 205

Sheppard, Nancy, *see* Nicholson, Nancy
spears, *see* kulata

Tangentyere Artists Gallery 195
TARNANTHI: Festival of Contemporary Aboriginal and Torres Strait Islander Art *123*, *131*
tawara camp 21, 24–7
Tent Embassy, Canberra 193, 195
terra nullius 32, 75, 166–7
Thompson, Punch Kawaki 141, 148, *156*, *159–60*
Tjukanku, Whiskey *153*
Tjukurpa 1, 27, 32–45, 51, 58, 65–6, 78, 122–5, 140, 164–5, 177–8, 191, gatefold
Tonkin, David 140–1, *155–6*, *160–1*, 175
Toyne, Phillip *159*, 171–2, 177
Turner, Lucy 6, 11, *11*

Uluru (Ayers Rock) 141, 170

Vestey Brothers 193

Ward, Nura 148
Watarru 190
water sources 28, 33, 36, 42, 74
Watson, Tjunmutja Myra *150*, 151
Wave Hill Walk-off 195
whirlwinds 74–5
Whitlam, Gough 193, 195
Whitlam government 157
Williams, Atira Atira Michael *13*
Williams, Maringka *13–14*
Williams, Mumu Mike
  biography viii, 200
  early life 4–29
  Hetti Perkins on 192–5
  on land rights 164–7, 169
  painting of 50–71, 77
  photographs of 5, *14*, *29*, *53*, *75*, *77*, *84*, *92*, *118*, *123*, *131*, *164*, *169*
  on Tjukurpa Law 32–45
  working on mailbags 90–118, 165
  writing of 74–84, 90, 165
Williams, Yilku Mulayangu Harry *5–6*, *14*
Wilson, Mantatjara *142*, 143
Wintawata No. 16 138
writing 74–84, 90, 165

Yankunytjatjara people 178
Yirrkala Bark Petition 194
Yolngu land claim 193
Young, Amanyl *19*
Young, Frank *19*, *164*, 167, 169, *169*, 172–3, 201
Young, Stanley *164*, *169*, 170, 172–3, 204

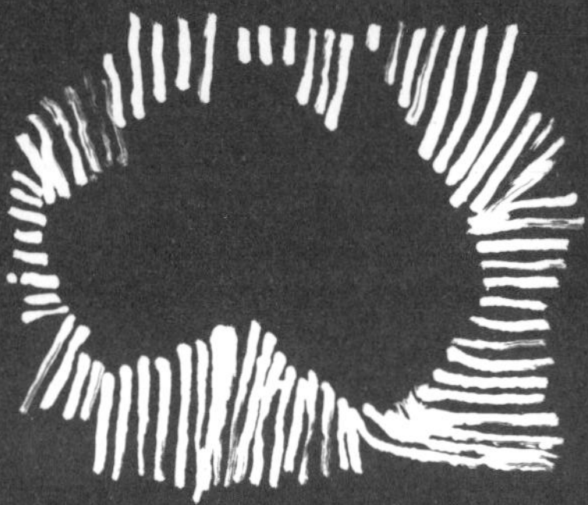

Ngurkatanama
Tjukurpa Munu Manta
Anangu Maru Tjutaku
nyangatja

Manta Nganampa
Tjukurtjara Munu Kunpu
alatjitu ku Tjupangk Ngurpengku
Putu Upani Ku kunpu
ngaranyi
Manta

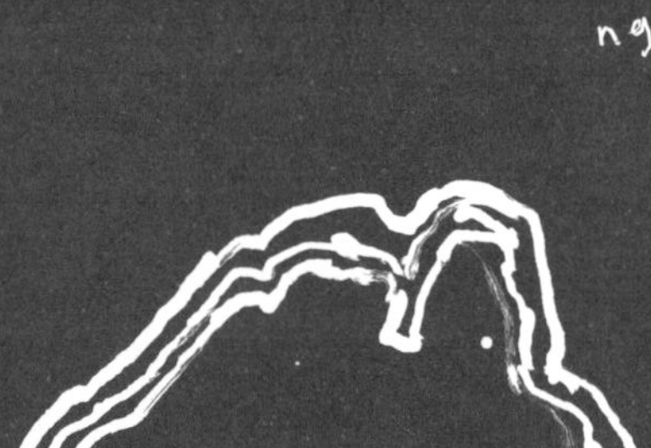

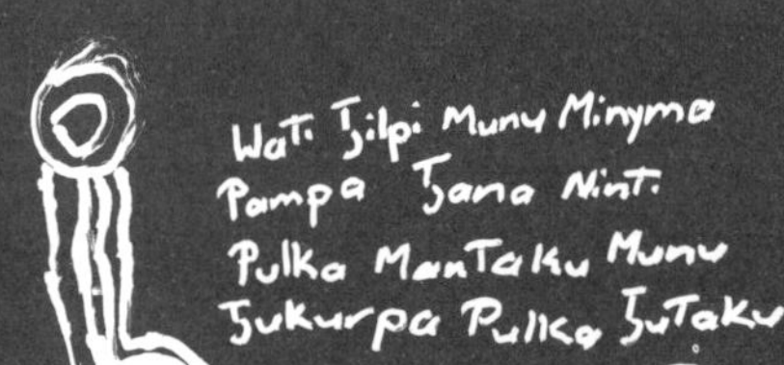

Wati Tjilpi Munu Minyma
Pampa Tjana Ninti
Pulka MantaKu Munu
Tjukurpa Pulka Tjutaku